The Complete
RELIEF PRINT

John Ross

Clare Romano

The Complete
RELIEF PRINT

THE ART AND TECHNIQUE OF THE RELIEF PRINT, CHILDREN'S PRINTS, CARE OF PRINTS, COLLECTING PRINTS, DEALER AND THE EDITION, SOURCES AND CHARTS

THE FREE PRESS
A Division of Macmillan Publishing Co., Inc.
NEW YORK

Collier Macmillan Publishers
LONDON

To Christopher and Timothy

THE FREE PRESS
A Division of Macmillan Publishing Co., Inc.

866 Third Avenue, New York, N.Y. 10022

Collier-Macmillan Canada Ltd.

Library of Congress Catalog Card Number: 74-2694

Printed in the United States of America

printing number
1   2   3   4   5   6   7   8   9   10

ACKNOWLEDGMENTS

We are indebted to a number of people whose energies and interest served to help our own. Many artists gave their time and knowledge in their special areas. They include Fritz Eichenberg, Andrew Stasik, Ansei Uchima, Lynd Ward, Antonio Frasconi, Toshi Yoshida, Carol Summers, Herman Zaage, James Lanier, Michael Ponce de Leon, Herbert Youner, Robert Blackburn and David Finkbeiner.

The basic manuscript was copy edited by Linda Mattison, whose suggestions were thoughtful, constructive and gratefully received. Marie Nolan patiently typed the major portion of the text with assistance from Mary Thompson. We wish to thank Sarah Sprague for compiling the index and checking the photos and captions. Douglas Howell demonstrated the process of making rag paper. Irvil Sloan of Multiples, Donna Stein of the Museum of Modern Art, and Elizabeth Roth of the New York Public Library were all willing with their time and expert help. Sylvan Cole and Aldis Brown, Estelle Yanco, Hilda Castellon, Candace Brown, Barry Walker, of Associated American Artists were generous in their assistance; Andrew Fitch and Walter Bareiss, both kind hosts as well as dedicated collectors, were pleasant and informed and shared their enthusiasm with us. Theodore Gusten of I.G.A.S. was cooperative and patient, as were Edna Blank of Andrews/Nelson/Whitehead, and Elke Solomon of the Whitney Museum. Timothy and Christopher Ross were willing models, printers, photo technicians and general assistants. Most of the photographs and all of the drawings are by John Ross, except where noted in the captions. Modernage Photographic Services processed the bulk of the photographs, both in black and white as well as in color. Our special thanks to Lewis Falce, President of Algen Press, for his interest and care in printing the color sections, and to Murray Printing Co. for their fine black and white work.

PRODUCTION CREDITS

This book was designed by Sidney Solomon,
who also planned and supervised the
production through all its stages.
Picture layouts: Bob Vari and Pete Landa
Typesetting: V & M Typographical, Inc.
Printing and binding: Murray Printing Co.
Color printing: Algen Press Corp.

PREFACE

This book is compiled from our larger work, *The Complete Printmaker,* which developed out of our interest in collagraphs in the mid nineteen-sixties. After several assignments as artists-in-residence with the U.S.I.A. exhibition "Graphic Arts U.S.A." in Yugoslavia and Romania, we realized how much interest there was in new methods and approaches in printmaking. There seemed to be little published material on the newer techniques and our students constantly requested information about them. Fellow artists and art historians from various parts of the country wrote to us for details concerning the collagraph, helping to convince us to write down our methods and experiences. Sidney Solomon, whom we first met when he was Director of Design for the Macmillan Company, was involved with the Free Press at that time. He saw our new work and was excited with the new direction and experiments. He prodded us to put some material together for a book on our use of this new technique. He became our editor, designer, and production director, and it was only through his constant interest and encouragement that this book has become a reality.

The emphasis in this presentation is on the workshop approach to printmaking. This postulates that one learns best by doing, and that a flexible approach is more productive than a highly structured, dogmatic sequence of problems designed to impart information in an academic way. The student develops his own ideas at the pace that suits him. An individual artist selects the method that best suits his esthetic intention. It will be helpful to him if he understands the possibilities of other techniques, so that his range of expression can be expanded when necessary. The diversity of work that takes place in a workshop atmosphere is stimulating to many artists, and can create an exciting environment for new and experimental projects. The possibility of combining techniques in a mixed-media statement is enhanced when working in a shop where many methods are being exploited simultaneously. Though small groups are better than very large groups, too few people are also a disadvantage. There should be enough activity in the shop to stimulate ideas and pro-

voke reaction to new directions. In this kind of situation the organiza
tion and planning of the workspace is of prime concern; thus we include
diagrams and photos.

The present intensity of interest in the fine print is directly related to
the advancement of technology in this century. A whole battery of new
materials and procedures is open to the adventurous artist who wants to
expand his imagery into the world of prints. The print is changing in its
technology and, therefore, in its expressive power. The magic of the print
becomes that much more intensified with the expansion of means. The
artist who is interested in these possibilities must learn to exploit the
new procedures and techniques to his advantage.

CLARE ROMANO
JOHN ROSS

CONTENTS

Section III   CARE OF PRINTS

Section IV   COLLECTING PRINTS

Section V   THE DEALER AND THE EDITION

Section VI   SOURCES AND CHARTS

BLACK & WHITE REPRODUCTIONS

COLOR REPRODUCTIONS

all following page 10

FOREWORD

The field of creative printmaking has a rich and varied history of development from its inception to the present time. Yet no period in history can equal the vitality and diversity of growth which has taken place in printmaking in the past twenty years. This growth has been characterized by a myriad of innovative processes and techniques, dynamically new and challenging materials, specially designed hand and power tools, new and better designed presses and most importantly this new interst in the printeed image has atracted an ever-increasing numbr of gifted and dedicated artists throughout the United States.

The full intensity of this growth and development in printmaking has been captured and recorded from the broadest general concept to the minutest significant detail in *The Complete Printmaker*. This excellent definitive volume is the cooperative effort of two highly respected members of the printmaking profession, John Ross and Clare Romano. Both authors have international reputations as creative artists gained from over twenty years of high level production, extensive exhibitions, travel and work abroad and a resultant impressive list of honors and professional recognition. They have played a vital role in the progress and development of printmaking in the United States as artists, teachers and officers in one of this country's most important print organizations, The Society of American Graphic Artists.

I am especially pleased to write this foreword to these special sections of *The Complete Printmaker*, made available in paperback form.

It is most fitting and gratifying that all these meaningful experiences should come together in the form of these volumes dealing with so many aspects of the fine art of printmaking. They are of ultimate value to the professional as well as the novice covering all the major categories of media in explicit detail. There is careful concern for the traditional approach as well as the newest and most inventive. Materials, tools, equipment, processes and techniques are all investigated and defined. The care and collection of fine prints is discussed in fullest detail as is the situation which surrounds the dealer and the establishing and distribution of the edition which so often confounds so many people.

Of invaluable assistance to anyone interested in purchasing tools, materials or equipment or the organization and implementation of a print workshop are the sections devoted to sources, charts and workshops. These sections contain complete, accurate and detailed information on all the necessities for the various media of printmaking and where they may be purchased.

One of the great pleasures of the book is a generous number of exceptionally fine photographs both in black and white and color which are visually exciting and add greatly to the edifying powers of the book.

The premise of these editions is based on the workshop approach—one learns by doing. The workshop environment also promotes a catholic approach to the solution of visual problems in the making of imagery. This book subscribes to the strength of specific or individual media and technique, but it also makes the sense of discovery and the rewards of combining media and techniques clearly apparent.

My friendship and professional involvement with John Ross and Clare Romano is of long standing. This has given me a privileged point of view from which to observe the growth of this book. The work has been long and tedious, but the results are most rewarding.

This is an excellent book which will add immeasurably to the further growth, development and understanding of printmaking. I am honored to give it my own professional approval by this introduction.

Rudy Pozzatti
Distinguished Professor of Art
University of Indiana, Bloomington

THE RELIEF PRINT

The Woodcut

INTRODUCTION AND HISTORY

Of all the forms of expression in printmaking, the woodcut is the most ancient. Its early beginnings in Egypt and China came from the use of wooden stamps designed to make symbolic or decorative impressions in clay and wax. With the development of paper on the Chinese mainland in the second century A.D., the stamping devices gradually evolved into wood blocks.

As plank wood was utilized by the artist and the craftsman, he was able to cut and print more sophisticated and complex designs. Many of the earliest images were for popular Buddhist religious use.

The woodcut came to Japan from China, in the wake of Buddhism, in the sixth century A.D. The early Japanese woodcuts were also religious in subject matter. It was not until the 17th century that a more highly developed art began to come forth. The Japanese printmaker's concept of the symbolism of subject matter, asymmetric composition, the use of flat color, pattern, and line were a great influence upon the work of Gauguin, Van Gogh, Lautrec, Whistler, and others.

The woodcut in western art evolved as a later expansion of the utilitarian printing of textiles from wood blocks used extensively in the early 14th century. Though paper from the east was known in Spain in the 11th century, it was not until paper was produced in large quantities in France, Italy, and Germany in the 14th century that the art of the woodcut began to unfold. In southern Germany, woodcuts began as primitive religious figures. Their directness, simplicity of line, and economy of means made them very powerful. They were handbills for veneration, sold for pennies to pilgrims visiting holy places and to the populace on religious feast days. Woodcuts of Christ or the Virgin Mary were often pasted inside traveling chests or onto small altar pieces and frequently sewn into clothing to give protection from evil forces.

As the invention of printing from movable type became a reality in the mid-15th century, the woodcut began to appear in more highly developed forms as illustrations for religious

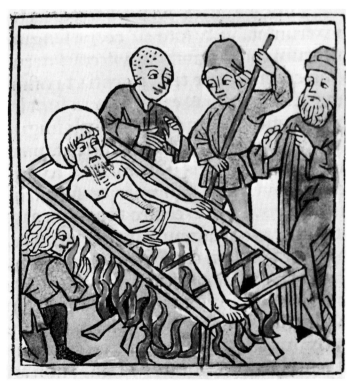

Jacobus de Voragine
Martyrdom of St. Lawrence, ca. 1474
From Legenda Sanctorum (Golden Legend)
Brooklyn Museum

1

books. By the late 15th century the great artists of the time, Durer and Hans Holbein in Germany, Lucas von Leyden in the Netherlands, and Titian in Italy were using this new medium with great eloquence.

After the mid-16th century, the woodcut began to decline in importance as a vehicle for esthetic expression. The richness and flexibility of line engraving and etching attracted most of the major artists dealing with the print. The woodcut and, later, the wood engraving became a means for reproducing popular painters and was used extensively for book, magazine, and newspaper illustrations. It was not until the revival of the woodcut as a sensitive, personal art form in the late 19th century, that it regained its place as a major expressive form. The prints of Gauguin, strongly influenced by the Japanese prints being exhibited in Paris, the prints of the German Expressionists who were returning to the simplicity of the early German Medieval woodcuts, and the prints of the Norwegian expressionist Edvard Munch greatly helped to renew interest in the woodcut as a serious contemporary art form. With this revival of the woodcut as a fine print medium came a new spontaneity and creative use of the material.

Until the late 19th century the woodcut was in a sense reproductive. The woodcuts of the German Renaissance, including those by Durer and Holbein, had often been cut by

Emil Nolde
"The Doctors" 1922
Woodcut 19⅞" x 27¾"
Dain Gallery, New York

highly skilled craftsmen from drawings made by the artists directly on the blocks. The prints became very fine facsimiles of exquisite pen drawings, having little relation to the quality of the wood. Line became the important element, mass or wood grain was rarely used. However, the artist-craftsman system, with the artist doing the creative work and the craftsman the cutting, enabled Durer and his contemporaries to produce a tremendous number of prints. Japanese printmakers also developed the same system. The artists designed the images, and the skilled craftsmen cut and printed the blocks. In succeeding years, with the artist so removed from the wood and the creating in less gifted hands, it was inevitable that the print became a reproductive image until the new approaches of the late 19th-century artists.

Because the contemporary artist uses the wood more freely with a real sense of the material and usually cuts and prints his own blocks, a more complete knowledge and respect for the material's potential comes forth. The aesthetic freedom of the 20th-century artist has enabled him to make new discoveries through experimentation and given him a richer utilization of the medium.

WOOD FOR RELIEF PRINTS

Pine

The most commonly available wood suitable for the technique of the woodcut is pine. It is soft, easily bruised, and requires very sharp tools if it is to be cut cross grain. Clear pine costs about twice as much as common pine but offers no knots. It is possible to buy pine boards up to 18" in width and occasionally up to 24", but larger sizes must be joined by edge gluing, which requires special clamps. Because of pine's softness, lines that are too thin are rounded or bruised in printing; in general, it is not a suitable wood for fine black line work. Sometimes it is advisable to coat the wood with a thin layer of shellac and sand it when it is dry. Thin the shellac with 50% alcohol to help it penetrate. It will harden the surface and make cutting easier. The wood is sometimes oiled to help prevent warping. Linseed oil may be used, but it should be applied some time in advance of cutting to allow the wood to dry.

Poplar

A medium soft wood with good cutting characteristics and even grain and not brittle is available in many lumber yards as whitewood (poplar); it is used extensively in inexpensive furniture. Poplar is slightly harder than pine and therefore it is possible to cut a little more detail on it. It is also used as backing wood for blocking copper or zinc line cuts and photoengravings. In the larger cities it should be possible to buy poplar blocks from the same manufacturer who supplies these backing blocks. It can be obtained type high (.918" thick) if enough is ordered to warrant a change in the planing machine. These type-high blocks may be printed on a Vandercook or other printing press (as discussed in section on press printing). Because poplar blocks are normally made from two or three inch strips, edge glued, they will not warp and they tend to retain a level surface.

Cherry and Pear Wood

These fruit woods are hard and dense and are suitable for very fine lines and long printing. Cherry blocks were, and still are, used by the traditional Japanese cutters in the Ukiyo-e tradition because of their resistance to splitting, their even grain, and their ability to withstand printing pressure and abrasion. Cherry is used for backing photoengravings even more often than poplar, and it is more easily available than poplar from blocking manufacturers. Pear wood is readily available in Europe but is a hardwood specialty item in the United States. It is quite similar to cherry in its characteristics.

Other Woods

Maple is so hard and dense that it is difficult to cut, but it yields extremely fine detail when properly worked. Oak is hard, stubborn, and full of a characteristic open pore texture that is disturbing. Mahogany is soft, very brittle, and has an open, pecky pore surface that is monotonous. Spruce and hemlock are soft, brittle, and mushy but can be used for color areas and knotty textures. Fir and redwood are brittle and flake off and chip when cut.

Plywood

When large areas are to be cut, plywood is the only answer. Fir plywood has a characteristic wild grain that is very dominating and hard to manage. However, pine plywood and gum plywood when available are quite usable for large woodcuts. Bass wood is also good. Cedar is too brittle to cut well. Birch is hard and has good even grain. A good birch plywood prepared for woodcutting is available from a Chicago supplier listed among the sources in the back of the book. Walnut is very hard, expensive, and has enough density to take fine even lines.

As many kinds of wood may be used in making woodcuts, the artist will choose that available wood which best suits the image he is cutting. Even old, worn, discarded boards are usable. Some artists save boxes full of old box wood, charred or burned pieces, knotty or rough sawn logs, and other wood which may yield interesting textures and shapes. With the correct procedure any piece of wood can be made to yield a good print.

WOODCUT TOOLS

A sharp nail will scratch the surface of a wood block, and the scratch will print as a white line on a black ground. Almost any object that is harder than wood will bruise or indent it, causing the indentations to print as white marks. Hard pencils will score most woods; paper clips will impress the surface; keys, tin cans, screwdrivers, needles, screws, dental tools, forks, pizza cutters, and plastic swizzle sticks will leave their impressions on the receptive surface of a piece of wood. All these implements can be used by the artist to create textures and designs that will print by the relief process. However, when good control of a shape or an area is needed, the knives and gouges come into their own and demonstrate why they have been used for so many years.

Objects that may be hammered or impressed into soft wood: A. Small brads. B. A leather punch with cross design. C. A hexagonal nut. D. A washer. E. Circular chuck. F. Staples.

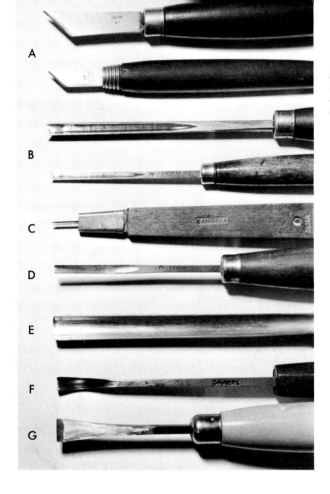

A

B

C

D

E

F

G

Some of the basic tools in woodcutting are shown top to bottom: A. Woodcut knives in two sizes. B. Raked V gouges, large and small. C. Small Japanese C gouge with movable steel gouge. D. Small shallow scoop or gouge. E. ⅜″ C gouge. F. Unusual rectangular gouge. G. Fish-tailed straight chisel.

Hold the knife as shown above. Make the first cut at about a 45° angle.

Turn your knife to the opposite side. Make the second cut, again at a 45° angle. The sliver of wood should curl up out of the cut. This method is for broad, fast cutting of large forms.

To cut smaller shapes and details, hold the knife somewhat like a pencil. Push it with the thumb of your other hand.

Turn the knife to the opposite angle. When you make the second cut the small sliver of wood should be loosened. Inside corners are easy to cut with a sharp knife.

The Knife

The knife has long been considered one of the prime tools of the woodcut artist, and justifiably so; it can perform cuts that no other tool can make and is one of the most useful instruments in the woodcutter's kit. It should be made of the best quality carbon steel, raked back from the point at about a 45° angle, and kept very sharp on the arkansas stone. The edge should be sharpened so that it is straight, not rounded; the point must be precise and keen if any small cutting is to be accomplished. There are many different sizes and styles of handles; choose one that is comfortable and workable and grips the knife blade very tightly so that it does not twist or wobble.

A few simple techniques will help you properly to cut with the knife. For broad cutting of large masses and long shapes hold the knife to cut at an angle of 45° to 60°. It takes four cuts with the knife to make one black line; in order to minimize the constant turning of the block that would be necessary if you held the knife at a constant angle you should learn to make the second cut by swinging the knife to the other side in order to release the cut splinter. Do not cut too deeply or you will tire quickly, and the fluency and responsiveness of your line will be impaired.

The knife is unexcelled for the clean cutting of inside small shapes where great control and accurate joining of lines is required. The tip of the knife does the most careful work. For this kind of cutting the tool should be held somewhat as a pencil between the thumb and the forefinger and be twisted and turned in the direction of the cut. As you can see the forefinger of your other hand can be used to push the knife into the wood and can be a great help, when your hand and arm are not strong enough to maintain the right pressure.

The depth of cut does not have to exceed ⅛″ except in large areas. This block has been cut by Antonio Frasconi.

Antonio Frasconi uses a small scoop to clear out an area on a block. Most of these tools are of Japanese manufacture.

Frasconi pushes the gouge with both hands for maximum control.

In addition to the traditional cutting, the knife can be used to achieve linear and textural qualities. It may be used to score the wood to create very fine lines either across the grain or with the grain. The knife can be used to bring up the grain if you hold the blade perpendicular to the block and scrape against the grain. It can be used as a chisel to shave away the wood. Its point can develop dot tones. Some very proficient artists use the knife as their only tool for all kinds of cutting, including cleaning out large areas of wood. However, other tools such as gouges and chisels are more efficient for this purpose.

Gouges and Chisels

You should have several kinds of gouges and chisels in your tool box. The most useful gouge is called the raked V gouge; when it is properly sharpened it will cut cross grain without tearing and is a joy to use. You can buy raked V gouges in various sizes from E. C. Lyons in New York City. It is handy to have two or more raked V gouges, the smaller one for detailed lines and the larger one for gouging areas and coarser textures.

A C gouge is indispensible for general cutting, and many sizes and shapes are available. When the curve of the gouge is very deep it becomes a U gouge and must be sharpened to a razor edge to cut effectively. There is an artist in Romania who has made over 1000 woodcuts in the past 30 years using almost exclusively a small C gouge for the entire image on each block. When any tool is used to this degree it makes the textures monotonous, and the forms themselves become constricted by the limits of the tool. Certain shapes and areas demand different tools, and for sensitive work it is necessary to have at least 3 or 4 varieties of gouges at hand.

A small flat chisel is a very helpful tool for getting soft grey edges when you do not want the typically hard-cut edge that is so characteristic of the woodcut knife or gouge. Study Antonio Frasconi's subtle and effective use of the flat chisel, and see the prints of Gauguin for soft edge effects.

Inexpensive Japanese Tools

The cheap sets of Japanese woodcut tools widely sold in the United States are useful for certain kinds of work. Although the steel is very soft and will not hold an edge for any length of time, the small knives are good for detail work, and the gouges will cut well for a while. Munakata uses them until they are dull and then throws them away. However, the greatest value of these tools lies in their ability to demonstrate the cuts that a certain type of tool will make before you spend a lot of money on a good quality tool. By testing the cuts of certain shapes of gouges and chisels you can determine which tools are best suited to your work and then buy a good high-carbon steel tool of that shape. As the cost of a complete set of twelve Japanese tools is less than $2, you can save the entire price with the discreet purchase of two good tools.

In any case, your tools should be kept in a tool kit or in a canvas tool roll in order to protect them and to keep them available.

Large wood cutting gouges and chisels can be stored in a canvas kit.

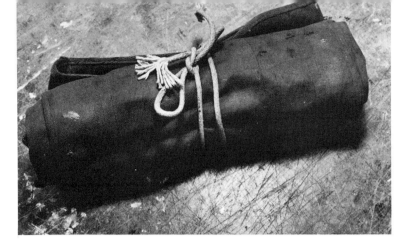

Rolled canvas tool kit. This type of storage is better for the cutting edges than throwing all the tools into a metal box where they slide around.

Sharpening

It is easy to resharpen your old straight V gouges to the correct angle of rake as shown on the diagram. Grind the tool to the desired angle on a coarse carborundum stone or on a small grinding wheel. If you use a wheel, do not overheat the tool or you may lose the temper in the steel. Once the correct angle is obtained, sharpen each side of the V gouge as you do a knife, making sure that the two edges meet at exactly the right angle. This point does the cutting, and it must be precise and true for the most delicate work.

The curved gouges are very difficult to sharpen, and it will take a great deal of practice and patience to master the technique. Hold the tool as shown and slowly turn the tool between your thumb and forefinger while keeping the same angle of tool to stone. It will take a number of turns before the edge can be ground evenly. The edge of the gouge should be rotated in small circles on the stone. When the tool is held in front of a light the edge should not be visible. If it reflects light on any one spot that area will need more stoning. There are a number of stones, both india and carborundum, with concave indentations of various curvatures for different-sized gouges. These are helpful to the beginner but scorned by old timers, who still insist that the flat stone is sufficient and the human hand is the best instrument for controlling the tool. Use enough fine oil to lubricate the stone and float off the tiny particles of steel that eventually will clog the stone. Pike oil, Three-In-One, or any light machine oil will work. Do not use linseed oil.

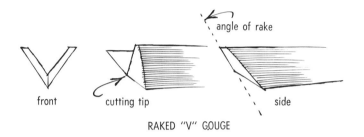

RAKED "V" GOUGE

To sharpen a curved gouge keep the angle of bevel steady. Move the gouge in small circles, rotating the shaft of the tool between the fingers.

CUTTING IN RELATION TO IMAGE

If the beginning woodcutter experiments freely with a variety of tools, he will begin to develop a preference and feeling for certain tools. Through selectiveness and growing experience in cutting, a personal manner in handling the tools will show itself, much as style develops in handwriting and drawing.

A good way to start to familiarize yourself with the tools is to prepare a series of small blocks without planned image. These blocks should exploit many cutting and texture possibilities inherent in the tools. By freeing yourself of imagery and finding out what the tools can do in the hand, you will

develop a basic cutting vocabulary and also understand the vast potential for tonality through textures. These experimental blocks can then be rolled up and printed to create a guide to future cutting.

Cutting methods, of course, vary in relation to the idea expressed. A good guide is to cut in the direction of the flow of the form. However, with images as varied and personal as they are in contemporary expression, any fixed rules would be impotent. One sure caution, however, is to avoid overcutting and to undercut wherever possible. It's easy to become carried away with the physical movements of cutting and to forget that each cut will appear as a white area. This is why undercutting and proofing are so important. Developing the block through the proofing is as important as the cutting on the block. If frequent proofs are pulled in developing stages and the proof is worked on with white paint to see how new areas will evolve, or with black paint to remove cutting, a freer concept can develop. Do not hesitate to sacrifice the drawn image on the block to constant proofing. The image can be easily re-indicated, and it is far more time-consuming to have to correct the overcut block.

Another caution is to try to keep a certain consistency in the scale of cutting. Again, this would apply to certain imagery and not to others. For instance, in an abstract concept, the scale of cutting would not need to be consistent. However, if certain special qualities were to be introduced in relation to landscape or figurative images, the scale, the weight of cutting, and therefore the sizes of the gouges or cuts would be very important.

Developing tonality or greys through the black-and-white print can be achieved in a variety of ways. The early woodcuts of Durer never relied on texture or wood grain. Form and tonality was developed in his woodcuts as it had been

Edvard Munch
"The Kiss" (1902)
Color woodcut, block 18⅜" x 18⅚₆"
Collection, The Museum of Modern Art, New York
Gift of Mrs. John D. Rockefeller, Jr.

Opposite:
John Ross
"Commercial Street" 1963
Color woodcut 23⅛" x 16½"

Brass brush, flat knife, and sandpaper emphasize granular structure to extent shown.

A brass suede brush, made for cleaning shoes and leather clothing, can subtly accent grain. Run in the direction of the grain.

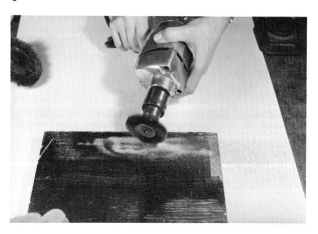

A steel wire brush gives a rapid, coarse texture.

The electric drill with a wire brush of brass will scour the surface of a block, accenting the grain.

conceived in his pen drawings. Today's expression in the wood is comparatively free. Line can of course express tone and form, but so can the great variety of textural cutting possible with the numerous cutting and textural tools used. Wood grain can play an extremely important role in the development of the image. Sometimes it has been used as almost the total image, as in Munch's *The Kiss*. Often it is the rich combination of grain, line, black mass, and texture that fulfills the wide potential of the wood.

Developing Grain

Many methods can be used to bring out the grain. When the image is expressed almost totally through the grain, a careful control must be exercised. One method is to hold the blade of a woodcut knife perpendicular to the block and lightly scrape the straight edge against the grain. Sometimes a thin scoring with your knife around the area where the grain is to be brought up will help you to keep within the form where strong grain quality is desired.

Where less control is necessary, a wire brush like an ordinary suede brush or a copper gun-bore cleaner is useful. In this method, the brush is rubbed with the grain.

Sandpaper in varying degrees of roughness may also be used, again rubbing with the grain. Pumice may be used in the same way.

A power-driven metal brush can be used if a rough texture is desired.

In all instances, the scraping, rubbing, or sanding wears away the soft particles of wood between the harder areas of grain, forcing the grain to become more prominent.

ROLLERS OR BRAYERS

Rollers present one of the greatest problems to an artist attempting the relief print. You will soon find that one roller will ink a certain block properly but will not work as well on another block. You will eventually need many different rollers, differing in size and in hardness of materials. There are a number of materials used in the making of rollers, ranging from gelatine, soft and hard rubber, composition, plastic, leather, and linoleum to lucite or plexiglas. It is necessary to understand what are the advantages and disadvantages of each type.

Hard Rubber Rollers

The small hard rubber rollers that are usually sold for use in printing linoleum cuts are of very little value to the serious printmaker. They are rarely of even diameter and ink an irregular, blotchy pattern at best. The most useful hard rubber rollers are made of cylinder rubber stock, which usually comes in outside diameters of 1½″, 2″, and 3″, and

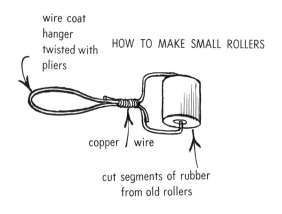

wire coat hanger twisted with pliers

HOW TO MAKE SMALL ROLLERS

copper wire

cut segments of rubber from old rollers

Antonio Frasconi
"Portrait of Sioux Chief Sitting Bull"
Color Woodcut 36" x 24"
Terry Dintenfass Gallery

Carol Summers
"Rainbow Glacier" 1970
Color Woodcut 36½" x 37"
Associated American Artists Gallery

Plate 1—*First Color*

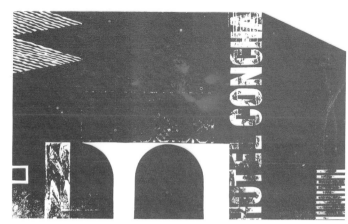

Plate 2—*Second Color*

Progressive I—*First and Second Colors*

Plate 3—*Third Color*

Progressive II—*First, Second, Third Colors*

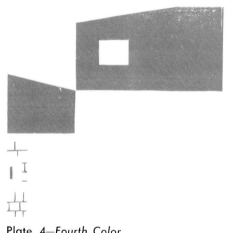

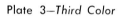

Plate 4—*Fourth Color*

Progressive III—*First, Second, Third, Fourth Colors*

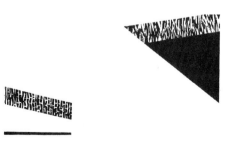

Plate 5—*Fifth Color*

John Ross
"Brokedown Palace" 1971
Cardboard reduction print 14⅛" x 20⁵⁄₁₆"

Ansei Uchima
"Cubes in Space" 1971
Color Woodcut 30" x 19¾"
Courtesy of the artist

Pablo Picasso
"Woman with Hat" 1962
Linocut 13¾" x 10¾" (reduction print)
Barney Weinger Gallery, N.Y.

with an inside diameter of ½", in lengths of 24". This material can be cut with a hand hacksaw or on a power saw with a hollow-ground blade, using a slow feed. The inside ½" diameter should be filled with a ½" maple dowel cut about ¼" longer than the length of the roller. This wooden core can then be drilled and mounted in a handle made from flat iron stock of approximately ⅛"-thick bar stock about 1" wide. If the iron bar stock is first scored with a hacksaw it will bend precisely at the proper place to fit the roller.

A hard roller of even diameter will ink the surface of a relief block without inking the shallow gouged or lowered areas. If you want a "clean" print without a lot of gouged texture, then a hard rubber roller is the proper choice.

Smaller rollers may be made with handles of stiff wire, such as the wire from coat hangers, bent into the proper shape with two pairs of pliers. As the most difficult part of the roller to make is the handle, it is desirable to save any suitable handle and simply replace the roller section. It is worthwhile to buy wallpaper rollers with a wooden or plastic roller and throw away the roller section. Then you may cut a section of cylinder rubber with a dowel insert to fit the handle section. The metal brackets may be bent inward to fit smaller rollers.

Soft Rubber Rollers

Soft rubber rollers are now obtainable from the Hunt Mfg. Co., Philadelphia, Pennsylvania, and are called speedball soft rubber rollers. They come in a variety of lengths from 1½" to 6". The smaller sizes are particularly handy for color areas. As the rubber composition is quite soft, they are useful for collage prints and for inking uneven blocks. They deposit ink on gouged areas in a very great amount and should be used with discretion. The rollers are too soft for blocks that are not very deeply gouged unless you want lots of gouging texture to print. They are also too soft for finely cut blocks, as thin lines fill in. The small diameter of these rollers is a handicap when you are inking a large area.

Gelatine Rollers

A very sensitive and useful brayer is made from gelatine. It gives a smooth, even distribution of ink. The disadvantages of gelatine are so numerous that it is rapidly being replaced by more durable materials. Gelatine pits very easily, melts in contact with water, will sag out of shape in very warm weather, will indent if left standing on a slab overnight, and is, in general, such a delicate and destructible material that it becomes very expensive to have your rollers recast every year, as is the custom in commercial printing shops.

Plastic Rollers

Soft plastic rollers are now being manufactured that combine the even inking qualities of gelatine with the more durable characteristics of hard rubber. They can be cast in an enormous variety of sizes and are the most useful rollers in the studio. As would be expected, these rollers are quite expensive. A 6" brayer with handle costs around $12. They are made of polyurethane or polyvinyl chloride and are very durable. They will withstand an amazing amount of abuse, and we recommend them highly. Large sizes are very expensive but are worth it.

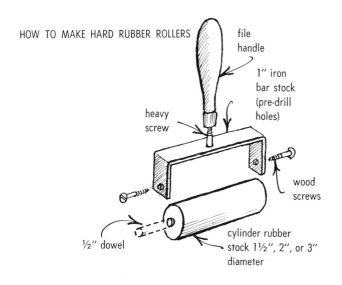

HOW TO MAKE HARD RUBBER ROLLERS — file handle — 1" iron bar stock (pre-drill holes) — heavy screw — wood screws — ½" dowel — cylinder rubber stock 1½", 2", or 3" diameter

Small rollers, many homemade, in varying sizes.

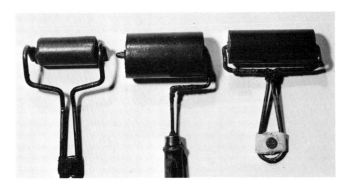

Cylinder rubber stock, available in 1½", 2", and 3" diameter stock, is very useful in the making of hard rollers. Handles can be made from coat hangers, wallpaper seam rollers, dowels, and the like.

An overhead roller rack is a great convenience when located over the work table. Rollers are always available and are out of the way when not in use.

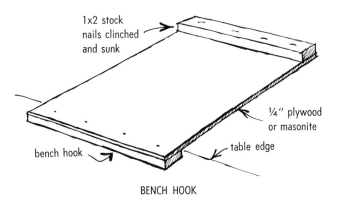

1x2 stock
nails clinched
and sunk

¼" plywood
or masonite

bench hook

table edge

BENCH HOOK

Bench Hook

A bench hook will hold the block from moving while the gouge is being forced through the wood. You can make a bench hook, using a piece of ¼" plywood, ¼" Masonite, or similar thickness composition board as a base. Glue or screw two pieces of 1"-thick wood on each end but on opposite sides of the base. Countersink the heads of the screws very deeply in order to avoid damage to the cutting edge of your gouge. One edge of the bench hook fits on the front of your table and the other side holds the block in position. It is a good idea to have several in various sizes because a small block simply won't work in a large bench hook.

C Clamps

You may clamp a large block to your table by using a carpenter's C clamp. The pressure of the threaded clamp will indent the block unless several layers of cardboard are used to protect the soft surface of the wood. Clamps are not as flexible as bench hooks because they must be loosened every time you want to move the block.

A bench hook holds the block in position and keeps it from sliding around when you gouge.

Gouging Jigs

Another useful tool is the gouging jig. If you are cutting a number of blocks it may be worthwhile to drill a number of ¾" holes in your table, spaced to receive ¾" dowels that have been glued to a strip of wood shaped as shown.

The right-angled corner is essential to keep the wood from slipping off the strip. The advantage of this method is that the holes may be drilled at the angle you prefer and the jig may be shifted easily to accommodate small blocks as well as large blocks.

The table on which you work must be either heavy enough not to slide all over the floor or prevented from moving by being placed against a wall or another piece of furniture. When a large amount of deep gouging is necessary, it may be helpful to use a small wooden mallet to help drive the gouge or chisel through the wood, particularly if you are working in a hardwood like cherry or pear.

Push the gouge with your right hand. The other hand acts as a guide and as a restraint against the tool and helps to keep it from slipping out of control.

The C clamp method of holding a block in position does not allow as much freedom of cutting as does the bench hook. Be sure to place a few pieces of cardboard between the block and the jaws of the clamp to prevent bruising the wood.

Texturing Tools

The soft surface of the wood may be indented or scratched by an enormous variety of things, from nails and screws to washers, bottle caps, punches, dog combs, drills, rasps, wire screening, and sandpaper. These can be hammered or tapped into the surface of the wood, and the indentations will print as white against the black surface of the block.

Multiple gravers made with a certain number of lines to the inch, ranging from 40 to 120 or more, are available from E. C. Lyons and E. C. Muller in New York City. These tools are made for photoengravers but are useful in the coarser sizes, i.e., 45-55-65, in obtaining closely textured grey tones. They work best with the grain.

Sculptors' tools, the small metal rakes with small teeth, also produce interesting textures.

Often a tool or implement designed for other purposes can work marvellously well. A dressmaker's sharp-pointed wheel for marking patterns, a little texture wheel for pastry mak-

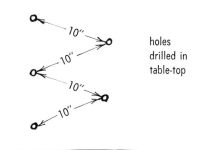

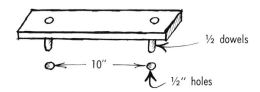

holes
drilled in
table-top

½ dowels

10"

½" holes

BLOCK SUPPORT IN TABLE
BY DRILLING HOLDS

Another method of keeping the block in position is to drill holes in your table top. Make a corner angle from an old canvas stretcher, insert two dowels through the stretcher, and fit the dowels into the holes in the table. If you make several holes you can adjust the angle to suit your block.

This shows the corner angle in use. The wood is held in place by the dowels, and the block cannot slip.

Ernst Kirchner
"Alpine Shepherd" 1917
Woodcut
Brooklyn Museum

ing, a sharp-edged pizza cutting wheel have all been useful tools in our studio. Look around you, in your workshop, basement, attic, kitchen, hardware or ten-cent store and discover texture-making tools that relate to your own images and you will introduce some freshness into your work.

Power Tools

Several types of power tools are very useful to the artist. The most easily obtained is the electric drill, which can be used with steel drill bits, wire brushes, and other tools. The block must be securely fastened to the table, or the force of the drill will move it around.

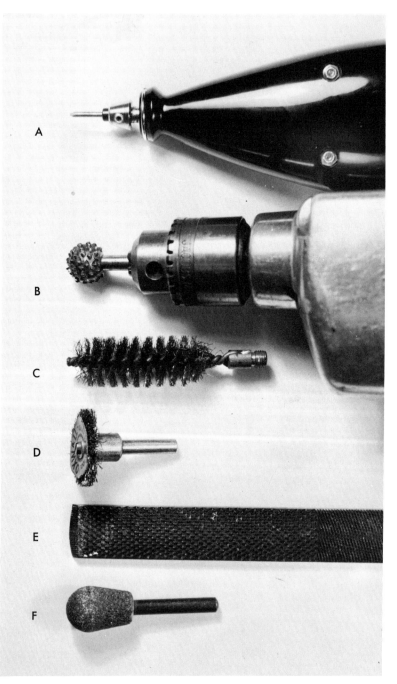

Auxiliary tools in woodcutting, top to bottom:
A. Multiple scratchboard tools, 40 lines to the inch. B. A screw-thread cutting tip that can make multiple grooves. C. An Exacto knife. D. A pie trimmer, which makes a zig-zag line. E. A glass cutter. F. A pattern wheel makes a dotted line. G. A leather punch for sewing seams. H. A sculptor's rasp makes multiple grooves. I. A dog comb, useful for coarse multiple strokes. J. A brass brush that can accentuate grain or texture the wood surface.

Other tools for texturing wood:
A. A motorized Vibro-tool which can be used on metal, wood, or plastic. B. An electric drill with circular bit. C. A brass gun cleaning brush. D. A wire brush for the electric drill. E. Wood rasp. F. A circular drum of carborundum.

A vibrating-point tool has been developed recently which has great potential if used with skill and care. There are several brands such as Vibro-Tool and Vibro-Graver. They can be used with a variety of points, from carbide or diamond tips to files and brushes. This tool is also useful for working in the intaglio methods on zinc, copper, or lucite plates. The stroke of the vibrating point is adjustable, and it can be used for many types of lines and textures.

A flexible shaft hooked up to a small electric motor is a very handy addition to an artist's workshop. There are a number of bits, grinding wheels, rasps, wire brushes, and other points that can be used.

All these tools are simply devices for easing the demands on the artist's strength and time. They are as much a part of a printmaker's equipment as the pencil or the knife.

Rubbing Tools

The choice of rubbing tool is often as personal as the choice of cutting tool. We have known artists to select from a wide range of objects hardly designed for printing use. These have ranged from an ordinary kitchen wooden spoon to the electric light bulb that a Romanian woodcut artist staunchly upheld as the best.

The traditional rubbing tool of the Japanese is the baren. It is a flat, circular disk backing a spiral of cord about 5½" in diameter covered with a sheath of bamboo. It is very sensitive for printing water-based inks. See the section on the Japanese method.

We have found a most useful rubbing tool to be two ordinary square wooden drawer pulls glued together. These may be purchased in many well-equipped hardware or 10¢ stores. One serves as a handle and the other as the rubbing tool. The handle can be selected for the size of the hand. The rubbing portion is usually most useful in the 4" dimension. Because the wood is quite raw, it is best to rub a little linseed oil into it in the beginning so that it glides easily over the back of the print and will not tear the paper. After a few printing sessions you will find a lovely patina developing. The flat of the knob is especially easy to use for large areas. The handle is excellent for small areas. Some of our students have fashioned their own tools by using a jigsaw and whittling a piece of wood to the desired shape.

Another excellent tool is a Japanese rice spoon made of bamboo. This can be purchased in a Japanese novelty shop for as little as 25¢. The flat end may be used for larger areas, the handle for smaller ones. Its great advantage is that it fits very comfortably in large and small hands. See the section on hand printing woodcuts.

The circular rasp produces a rough, uneven texture.

INKS FOR RELIEF PRINTING

The oil-based printer's inks normally used for the relief print are available from a large number of ink manufacturers. It is much easier to keep this ink in tubes than in cans. The small extra charge for the tubes is well worth it. However, as many colors are not available in tubes and can be obtained only in cans, it is good practice to replace the circular waxed-paper liner carefully, pressing it down and

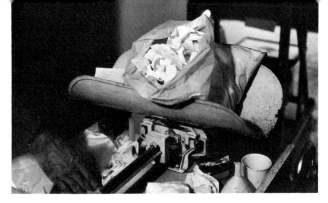

Douglas Howell weighs cotton rags on a scale to prepare the raw materials for paper manufacture.

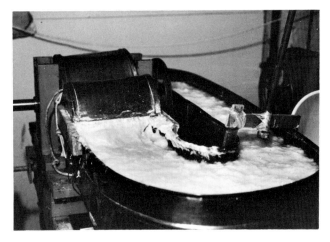

The rags are reduced to a pulp, called stuff, in the beater. Howell controls the length of the fibers by the duration of the beating.

The wire mesh screen or mold used to make each single sheet of paper. The water mark of copper wire is in the upper corner.

Below: The screen is immersed in the stuff to a certain depth, then it is removed as shown. It is shaken in two or more directions in order to interlock the fibers by Howell, acting as vatman.

leaving no air bubbles, before sealing the can with the lid. Wipe the rim clean, too.

The water-based inks are much harder to use because they dry so quickly. Oil inks are much more flexible and are preferable to water-based inks. However, water-based inks are discussed in a later section on the Japanese method. See section on color inks for relief printing.

PAPERS FOR RELIEF PRINTS

The wide variety of papers available to the printmaker working in the United States offers great flexibility and choice in every medium. The papers most suitable for printing relief blocks are handmade in Japan from the inner bark of the mulberry tree and other plants and bushes, such as the hibiscus and the hydrangea. Almost all the papers are used unsized and not dampened. Some of the characteristics of the most useful Japanese papers are listed in the chart on papers.

For very fine lines, such as in delicately cut wood engravings and relief etchings, it may be better to use machine-made papers. The handmade papers vary in thickness and have much more surface texture than most machine-made papers of rag content, and the fine detail is somewhat harder to print on rough stock. Many domestic papers are suitable,

The deckle is removed from the screen while excess water drains off.

Below: The pulp or stuff has been formed to the shape of the screen, making a sheet of paper.

including Mohawk text, Strathmore all rag Book in wove surfaces, and Strathmore bond wove. Some of the European papers are very good for fine detail in press printing. These include Basingwerk light, Arches text wove, Maidstone, Rives light wove, and Opaline, a parchment paper. Most of the imported papers can be obtained through Andrews-Nelson-Whitehead in New York or Aiko Company in Chicago, if ordered in quantity.

See the paper chart in the back of the book for further information.

PUTTING THE IMAGE ON WOOD

Painting on the Block

Wood lends itself exceptionally well to mass, both solid and tonal, and to the use of strong line. The density of the wood and the direction of the grain are factors to be considered in the planning of the image. If you keep this in mind, the preparation can be approached in a variety of ways depending on your esthetic direction and your needs as an artist. The inspiration for a particular image may vary considerably for each artist. Working directly on the block can be especially interesting. Take special care to select wood that has an interesting grain, knot, or rough-sawn texture that can help evolve the image.

One way to proceed is to paint directly on the wood surface with India ink, working with verve and speed. When the ink drawing is dry, tint over the block with a diluted oil-based ink, rubbed in with a rag. As an alternate method you can take the block (prepared with a thin coat of grey poster color, rubbed on with a rag, so that the wood will not become too wet nor the pigment too thick) with you as you would a sketch pad or drawing paper. You can paint directly on the block with a Japanese brush, a pointed sable, or a

The newly formed sheet has been couched on a stack of felts, called a post. The mold is removed with a rolling motion.

Below: The felts absorb moisture from the sheets and impart a texture to them. Douglas Howell makes only fine rag paper.

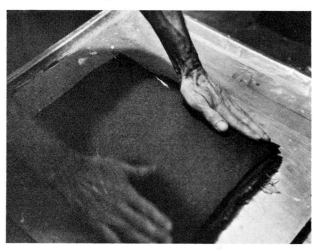

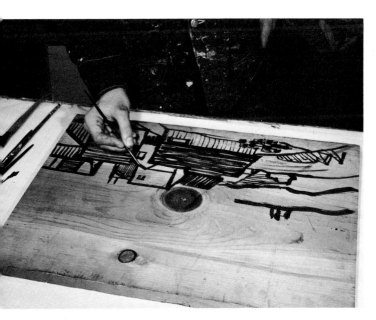

Painting directly on the block with india ink and brush is a good way to keep the image fresh and strong.

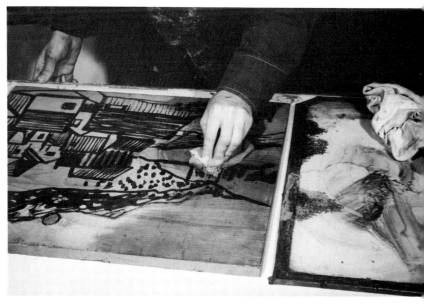

When the ink drawing is dry, tint the entire block with a dilute mixture of printers ink. Red, grey, blue, or some color of intermediate tonal value is rubbed over the drawing. Pour some varnoline or benzine on a rag, and thin the ink enough to tint the surface.

magic marker. Keep some of the grey poster color handy for making changes. You may use two instruments, a brush or pen with black to indicate positive forms and a brush with grey to make corrections. This method is extremely free and spontaneous. You may analyze the drawing back in the studio and develop it further just as you would a drawing on paper. Felt pens in a variety of sizes or speedball pens in an assortment are also very useful for attaining fluidity of line and quick development of mass.

Material for Painting on Block

India ink
Poster color—black and white
Brushes, flat and pointed and Japanese
Felt pens, assorted thin and thick sizes
Speedball pen nibs, #6 and #8
Sharpened stick, pen holder, or brush handle for stick drawing
Two mixing tins
Oil-based ink (red, blue, or grey)
Rags
Water
Wood, large 15″ or 18″ width of clear or common pine or poplar, ½″ or 1″ thick

Cutting Without Sketch

Another approach, related to the method just discussed, is cutting directly into the block without a previously prepared sketch. This is a very personal manner and seems to be most successful when the artist has a clear mental concept of his image. The block should be blackened with a rag dampened with India ink, diluted with a little water, so that the cut marks can be easily seen. The very act of cutting becomes an important part of the evolvement of the block. The physical motions themselves help to achieve a certain freedom. A student at Pratt Graphic Center worked on huge pieced planks or large drawing boards in this manner. He blackened his block with India ink and, with perhaps only a rudimentary positioning of forms with white chalk, would proceed to cut large expressionistic, figurative images with gouges and knives. However, the beginning artist of the woodcut must not confuse the size of the block or the gouge or the expressionism of the image with a result that will necessarily be free or spontaneous. Unless great control of design and composition and tool is part of the artist's experience, this method, if attempted without taking time to get the feel of the materials, can often result in large, impetuously cut blocks without enough organization. It is often better to start with medium-sized blocks and some planning.

Materials for Cutting Directly into Block

India ink, rag, mixing tin, water, white chalk
Wood, large 15″ or 18″ width of clear or common pine or poplar, ½″ or 1″ thick
Variety of cutting tools

Charcoal Offset Drawing

In this method, the drawing can be prepared in line on tracing paper with a compressed charcoal pencil, (a soft 6B

A very quick transferring procedure uses a drawing made with soft pencil or charcoal pencil. Do not fix the drawing. Turn it over, face down, on the block and tape it in position. Rub the back of the tracing with a spoon or a wooden drawer pull.

Below: If more pressure is needed rub the back of the tracing with your finger nail.

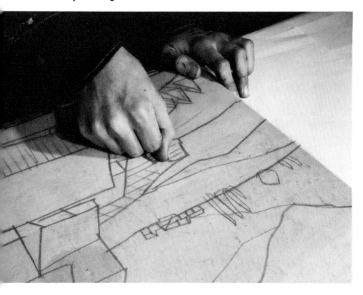

General's or Wolf's are very good), keeping in mind the need for simplicity and directness. The charcoal pencil should be used full strength without reliance on smudging effects. After the drawing is completed, it can be placed face down and taped to the block. The block should be tinted beforehand with sepia or grey poster color or printing ink diluted in varnolene, so that the cut marks will be seen easily. The back of the tracing is carefully rubbed with a rice spoon or drawer knob with strong pressure. The dense black compressed-charcoal pencil transfers itself quickly to the block with excellent readability. A good spray of fixative will keep the drawing from smudging, and cutting may begin. Any good brand of spray fixative such as Krylon or Blair may be used. Because the drawing is reversed when it is placed on the block, the finished print will read as the drawing was made on the tracing paper. There will not be a mirror image such as occurs when the drawing is painted directly on the block.

Tracing-Paper Transfer Method

In this method the drawing can be prepared on paper or illustration board in a manner that would relate well to the simplicity of line and mass of the woodcut. Use some instruments that have a relationship to the medium, such as brush or speedball pen and ink or felt pens. After the drawing is developed to your satisfaction, a tracing in mass can be made with a 6B General's or Wolf's compressed charcoal pencil, drawing every line and mass with the sharpened charcoal pencil. After the drawing is completed, it can be placed face down and taped to the block and rubbed with a rice spoon, a drawer knob, or your finger nail.

A variation on this method is to make a linear tracing of the prepared drawing with a medium soft pencil. The tracing is then placed face down with a piece of carbon paper between block and tracing. The block may also be prepared with a light tint, as described in the first discussion of the indirect method of preparing the image. The drawing may then be traced with a medium pencil so that the carbon paper deposits the image with sufficient strength onto the block. Be careful not to trace with too much pressure because the wood indents easily. This method is the least satisfactory because of the additional step required in the use of carbon paper and because tracing the linear image of a drawing is alien to the concept of the woodcut and becomes too reproductive.

Materials for Charcoal Offset and
Tracing-Paper Transfer Method

6B General's or Wolf's compressed-charcoal pencil
Tracing paper of very transparent quality
Medium H pencil
Carbon paper
Masking tape
Small spray can of fixative
Japanese rice spoon or wooden drawer knob for rubbing
Wood cut to size

Japanese Transfer Method

Still another transfer method is used by the Japanese traditionalists. It requires a carefully done tracing of your

The pencil drawing has been placed on the block. When the block is cut and printed it will be "flopped" back into its original position as on the drawing, a great advantage of this method. Lettering is easy to do by this method.

Another method for transferring a drawing is the carbon-paper technique. Tape a tracing of your shapes to the block. Slip a carbon-paper (typewriter carbon is O.K.) under the tracing and trace through the drawing so that it is transferred to the block. *Below:* Check the block. Use a soft pencil. A pencil that is too hard will indent the wood and those indentations will print as thin white lines.

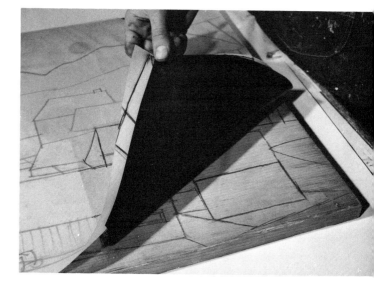

design. The process is described in the section on the Japanese method under "pasting the drawing on the block."

Proofing the Woodcut

Pulling an impression of the cutting, no matter how rudimentary it may be, is an important aspect in developing the woodcut. Proofs may be made without using ink at all. One useful method is to rub the raised cut surface thoroughly with a large stick of graphite. Place a piece of Troya proofing paper over the area and rub with a suitable rubbing tool. A clean, sharp, readable impression of the developing block should be visible. Observations and changes can be easily made right on the proof with white and black poster color if the graphite impression is sprayed first with some fixative. The graphite method is useful for small areas when the block is in very early stages. When cutting is more advanced, ink is more advisable. The graphite may be readily removed from the block by rubbing with a rag sprinkled with a small amount of varnolene. Another process is to place paper over the block and then to rub it with a stick of graphite to produce the image.

Another method of proofing is to roll up the block with a light even coat of black ink and again to pull a print on Troya paper. A useful method is to pull two proofs if there is to be some extensive correcting with black and white poster color on the proof. One proof with painted changes and one proof to show what exists on the block can be very helpful in finding the areas to be corrected.

Developing and changing the block through proofing eliminates a great deal of the hazard of overcutting and enables the artist to realize the potential of the wood in a clearer, faster way. The greatest surprise always seems to come after the beginner has lovingly cut the block, which becomes a thing of beauty in itself, a bas relief, where every cut seems to have meaning because of the texture of the wood and the play of light on the relief surface. Then with the first proof, the unhappy revelation comes: None of these nuances are evident! It becomes a flat relation of white line and mass against black. The whites are invariably cut too heavily, too deeply, and too much.

Cleaning the block without dirtying the recessions on the block can be achieved if only a dry rag is used to clean away the ink. If this is insufficient for proper cleaning, then a rag with just a few drops of varnolene should do the trick.

CORRECTING ERRORS IN RELIEF BLOCKS

Wood Blocks

It is rather difficult to correct mistakes in wood, and great care should be taken not to overcut your blocks or to damage areas that should print. However, certain things can be done to repair small damages and bruises. These methods have distinct practical value and will save many a damaged block.

Plastic Wood

The easiest and fastest method to repair broken lines, overcut textures, and general overcutting is to fill the area

It is possible to take a quick "proof" of a cut block by rubbing a piece of paper with litho crayon or pastel when it is positioned on top of the cut area.

with fresh plastic wood, applied in as many coats as necessary to fill the holes. Allow each coat to dry. Don't allow each layer to exceed a thickness of about ⅛". Apply plastic wood to rough, new wood that has not been soaked with oil or ink. A clean base is essential for the plastic wood to stick properly. If this is not possible, since most errors or the need to make changes are not discovered until after a proof is pulled, clean the block well with solvent, especially in the recessions, and dry it well with a clean rag. It often helps to roughen the surface to be repaired with scraping movements of a knife. This will help the plastic wood to bind to the block. The final coat should be slightly higher than the level of the block but not excessively high or it will be too time-consuming to lower the plastic wood back to level. Sand the high spots with fine sandpaper, wrapped around a rectangular block. Sand with the grain only, keeping the pressure even and working carefully in order not to damage the surrounding areas.

Plastic wood will not withstand rough treatment, and occasionally the material falls out, particularly if the inking brayers are gelatine. Press printing also tends to pick out loose areas of plastic wood. For long editions and permanent work it may be better to plug the block or to cut a new block. With plastic wood, it is relatively easy to fix spots that have not been too thoroughly gouged out. If a section has been completely ruined by excessive cutting and it extends over a large area, it may be preferable to try the next method.

Planing Areas to Correct Mistakes

When the offending section extends to the edge of the block, it may be better to plane the whole section down to fresh wood. This is radical surgery, indeed, and will work in only a few cases. Plane with the grain and go deep enough to expose enough good wood to allow for proper recutting. When you have finished planing, sand the entire area with fine sandpaper to even out the plane marks. A block treated in this way can be printed only by hand rubbing and will never print properly on a press.

Plugging

When a line or two has broken and the block must be printed for a long edition, the best repair method is to cut a plug of a wedge-shaped piece of wood several inches long. Cut a deep tapered groove through the line that is broken, removing all the wood to be replaced. Hammer the wedge into the tapered cut until it is forced in very tightly. Cut off the excess with a hacksaw blade, sandpaper down to the level of the block, and recut the line. The wedge will fit so tightly that it need not be glued. If you need a larger area than the wedge will cover, you can cut a block shaped to fit a deep incision in your block. The depth of the incision should be over ¼", and the sides should be cut vertically. This piece will have to be glued in position with Elmer's or carpenter's glue, sanded level, and then recut to gain the desired effect. The bottom of the incision should be level enough to have the glue hold the repair block in place.

It is possible to drill circular holes with a bit and then glue in pieces of wooden dowel to fit the drilled holes. This method does not make a good joint and can only be used for small, isolated repairs.

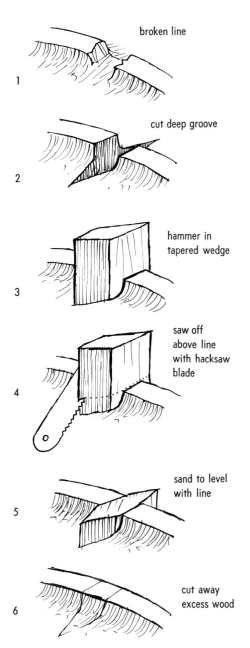

1 broken line

2 cut deep groove

3 hammer in tapered wedge

4 saw off above line with hacksaw blade

5 sand to level with line

6 cut away excess wood

REPAIR OF BROKEN LINES IN WOODCUT

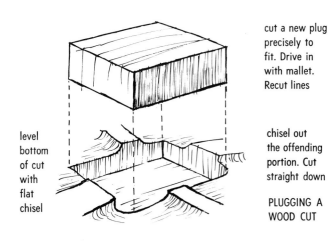

cut a new plug precisely to fit. Drive in with mallet. Recut lines

level bottom of cut with flat chisel

chisel out the offending portion. Cut straight down

PLUGGING A WOOD CUT

The brayer (or roller) should spread the ink evenly over the surface. Good distribution of ink is vital to a clean impression.

Ink the block thoroughly. Move the roller in many directions, building up the ink gradually. Too much ink will fill the fine textures and delicate cutting.

Below: Here a Japanese rice spoon, made of bamboo, is used as the rubbing tool. The flat side covers large areas quickly.

Repairing Other Relief Blocks

The repair of a relief etching is a rather tricky process. When a zinc plate is etched, it is often necessary to change poorly drawn or incorrect passages.

If this happens, scrape the entire area evenly to eliminate all ridges and bumps, turn the plate face down on a polished metal plate, such as an inking platen or ¼″ steel plate, protecting the face of the relief etching with newspaper, and hammer the back of the plate over the offending area until the zinc has been forced into the proper level again. You must hammer fairly vigorously, using a rounded hammer. With careful work you can force up a considerable amount of zinc and make repairs by re-etching the scraped out areas. Use wooden calipers to locate the proper spot to hammer on the back of the plate. This process is called repoussage.

A linoleum cut may be repaired easily. Simply cut the bad area out and reglue another piece of linoleum on the backing board. Cardboard collage and other collage relief plates are so easy to repair that this quality is a very positive factor in their wide acceptance and popularity. You can glue new pieces in position very quickly with any one of a number of good adhesives, such as polymer gesso, Elmer's glue, thickened lacquer, model cement, and the like.

HAND PRINTING

The printing of the woodblock is almost as important as the cutting. Without a doubt, sensitive printing through careful inking and rubbing can reveal all the nuances of line and tonality that may be inherent in a block. Heavy inking and a heavy hand at rubbing with an improper tool can make a sensitively cut block look inept.

A few careful steps that should be followed can help to produce prints with excellent printing quality. First, it is important to set up for printing. The cutting table should be thoroughly cleaned with a dust brush of all wood chips. The block should be brushed off with a soft wire brush to eliminate any possibility of tiny chips of wood clinging to the block and being picked up by the roller and redeposited onto the block. If these little chips become lodged between paper and block, rubbing the paper during printing soon produces tears in the paper and ruins a good print. All tools used in the cutting process should be put aside. Only the block, a tube of black printing ink, a palette knife, a slab for rolling, a good roller, one or two rubbing tools, and enough precut paper should appear on the work table.

A word might be said here about choice of roller and ink. The quality of softness or hardness of the roller is important in relation to the quality of the cutting. If the block is finely cut with considerable detail and tonality, then a hard roller and stiff ink is very important. If the cutting is in free large forms, a softer roller and less stiff ink may be used.

Squeeze a moderate amount of ink onto the slab. Pick up some ink on the roller and roll it out on the slab in horizontal and vertical movements. Be sure the ink is distributed evenly on the roller and the slab. When there is a thin even layer on the roller, begin to deposit it on the block in a variety of horizontal, vertical, and diagonal movements in order to distribute the ink evenly. This process can be repeated three or four times from slab to block until there is an even, tacky, moderate deposit of ink on the block. Avoid too much ink. Overinking will fill in thin lines and produce a too-thick uneven deposit on the paper.

When the block is properly rolled up, place the paper carefully on the block, leaving even, two-inch margins, and rub moderately with the palm of the hand to smooth out the paper and adhere it to the block. Rub with moderate to heavy pressure from the back, with the Japanese rice spoon or the wooden door knobs or whichever rubbing tool feels comfortable for you. Rub in small even strokes from the center of the block outwards, with consistent pressure rather than long, broad strokes that are more difficult to control. Hold the paper down with your free hand. Pick up a corner of the print, being careful not to disturb the registry, and check the quality of printing every now and then. If the paper is of a medium to thin variety, some of the imagery will show through on the back, which will often indicate that there is proper pressure and proper amount of ink. If the block has been too lightly inked it sometimes can be carefully reinked if the paper is picked up in small areas at a time, holding the adhered area down with the other hand, and the rerolling done without disturbing the registry.

Two hands give more pressure to the bamboo rice spoon, helping to give emphasis to certain areas of the block.

Place the paper in position, using a register frame if you want consistent margins. The register frame is optional for one color prints but essential for color register work.

Below: Rub the back of the print with good pressure. The rubbing instrument is two drawer pulls, glued together.

Use the edge of the spoon for greatest pressure and, therefore, the strongest impression.

Below: Check the printing by lifting the corners after you have rubbed the major part of the block. You can replace the paper and reprint the light areas.

Tonal qualities can be achieved through printing, and tones can vary in the same print, again through printing. If one area in a print is supposed to be black and another grey, rub the black area heavily with the rubbing tool, and in the grey area, rub lightly with just the fingers. Even more controlled greys can be achieved by inking lightly in some areas and more heavily in others and again using a combination of fingers and rubbing tool for printing.

PRESS PRINTING

The sensitive control that is possible when you are printing by hand-rubbing or spooning the back of the paper is a tiring, time-consuming operation. Some prints can be achieved only through this method. However, if you need a large edition or want to print the block together with type, it may be possible to plan the block for printing in a press. There are four or five types of presses that might be used.

Relief Printing on an Etching Press

The most commonly available press is the typical etching press, with a bed passing between two steel rollers. If the upper roller can be adjusted upward to one inch or more above the bed, you may easily print a woodcut on this type of press. The inking may be done with hand brayers or rollers. More than one color can be rolled onto the block if the areas to be inked are separated enough to avoid overlapping.

The block need not be perfectly level for printing on the etching press. Slight cupping or curling is no great disadvantage because the contact area between the steel printing roller and the inked block is a thin line, about ¼″ wide. This contact enables the block, even though warped, to print evenly if the block is placed on the press so that the grain runs parallel to the length of the press roller. Use a newsprint or other packing paper, such as a blotter to keep the blanket clean. Normally one blanket is plenty, and the pressure may be much lighter than that used for intaglio print-

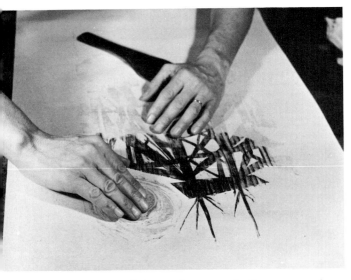

If you want very light tonality, use only the pressure of your fingers.

The finger-rubbed area is much lighter than the spoon-rubbed shapes.

An etching press may be used to print woodcuts if the roller can be raised high enough to accomodate the block. In this case the Brand press is equipped with springs for this purpose. Ink is applied with a brayer.

Below: Light packing is used for level blocks. Newsprint and a blotter are put under a thin blanket. The pressure is controlled by micrometer gauges.

ing. Now we are merely printing from the surface of the block.

Smoother papers tend to print more accurate detail and texture than rough papers. If you use thin Japanese papers such as Mulberry, Sekishu, or Moriki, the ink may be forced through these porous papers, soiling the blankets. Heavier stocks need less packing and are easier to handle.

Avoid handling the inked block while it is in position on the press bed. You may tape paper to the bed and mark, with a pencil, the corners where the block fits. It is easy to make little cardboard stops and tape them to the bed to indicate the precise position of the block. The paper may also be controlled in this way, making possible an even margin throughout the edition. When you are involved with color work, it is possible to have a color register system with taped cardboard stops.

Press printing yields longer editions than hand printing because the pressure is evenly distributed over the entire length of the block instead of being localized in small areas by the hand rubbing method.

Relief Printing on the Vandercook Press

Editions of several hundred or more in several colors are feasible if you can obtain the use of a Vandercook press for printing. There are many models, depending on size and inking facility. The older models are relatively cheap, because every printer had a press of this kind for proving his typographic matter. Many models have no inking rollers and the inking must be done with brayers, and only the impression is performed on these presses.

Some older Vandercooks have no grippers, and these presses are much more difficult to use for larger editions than models with grippers. It is possible to do color register work with gripperless presses by linking enough rubber bands to form two strings. These bands are wrapped around the cylinder and fastened with string or paper clips. The paper to be printed may be slipped under these rubber bands, taking care to see that the printing surface does not come in contact with the rubber bands, or it will be damaged. Mark the packing sheet with pencil as a guide for the paper, so that successive sheets may be placed in a similar position. The register obtained by this method is not as precise as that obtained by more recent presses.

These newer presses have inking rollers attached to the printing cylinder, and these rollers ink the block in the instant after the printing drum has passed over the block. Some presses have motor-driven inking rollers that automatically distribute ink over the surface of the rollers. These presses are ideal for longer editions.

Lock-Up on the Vandercook

The block must be fixed in position within the bed of the press, in order to prevent slipping and insure even margins. The easiest way to fix the block is to use an automatic lock-up bar, supplied by Vandercook in different lengths for the varying beds that are manufactured. They are expensive, however, and a 19-inch lock-up bar costs over $75.

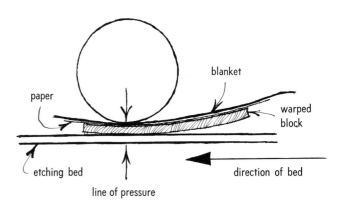

HOW TO PRINT A WARPED BLOCK ON ETCHING PRESS

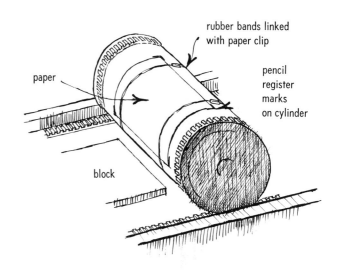

REGISTER CONTROL ON SIMPLE PROOF PRESS

To print an edition on the Vandercook 25 press, the block is locked in position using plywood furniture and conventional quoins. The block must be level.

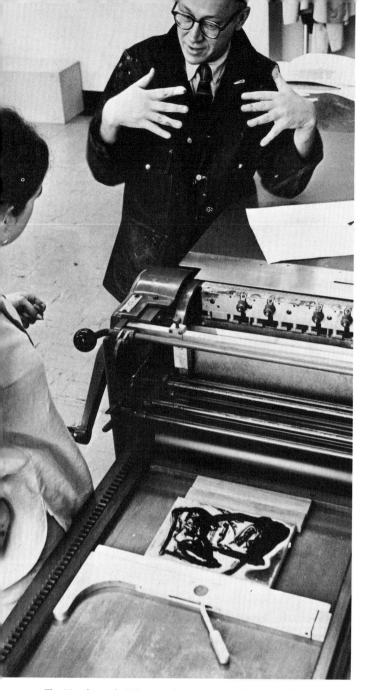

The cheapest lock-up is made with pieces of square wood, called furniture, held in place with keys and quoins. Wooden furniture is cheap, available everywhere, even secondhand, and most job printers get rid of their old furniture from time to time. Metal furniture is better than wood, and plastic furniture is better than metal but is very expensive and not yet commonly available. A great convenience if you do much press printing is to have some magnetic metal furniture handy. You may use this material to lock the block in position temporarily, for a few proofs. It is not suitable for a lock-up that is going to be printed for a large number of impressions.

Make-Ready on the Vandercook

If you use type-high (.918″) wood that is quite level, you will find good impressions are easy to obtain. Slight variations in printing surface may be remedied by gluing thin pieces of strong tissue paper (called make-ready) on the packing sheet over the printing cylinder. Use Sphinx paste, and if the edges of the paper cause a sharp line to print, sand the edges with fine sandpaper in order to smooth the edges. Better still, tear the paper instead of cutting it with scissors. This will usually solve the problem. It may be necessary to glue more than one level of make-ready paper to the packing sheet in order to bring the printing surface to proper height. Discard the packing sheet when the edition is finished. Don't attempt to reclaim it for your next print because it will be ruined by the glue.

If you use wood that is less than type high, slip a few sheets of thin cardboard or oak-tag under the block in order to build up the height of the block. Cut these sheets slightly smaller than the block so that they do not stick out and ruin your lock-up.

Wood that is warped or curled may present too much difficulty to print, and make-ready will not suffice to correct this handicap. Therefore, your blocks should be level from the start when printing on a proof press, because it is fixed in position and cannot adjust to the rollers as on an etching press. The best source of level blocks is from a manufacturer of backing wood for photoengravings. These blocks are usually of cherry or poplar, both very good for woodcuts.

It is possible to print from relief etchings made from zinc or copper plates or from collage plates made from cardboard, paper, cloth, and other materials. If these plates are to be press printed, care must be taken to get the surface of the plate as level as possible, otherwise the make-ready will be an enormous task. The collage plates should be well sealed and thoroughly glued in order to withstand the suction of the inking rollers and the pressure of the impression cylinder.

Printing on the Vandercook

The quality of impression possible from the Vandercook is excellent, depending upon the proper preparation of the make-ready and the right distribution of the ink. Too much ink will fill the fine texture of the block and clog the fine lines. It is better to start with a thin film of ink and build it up rather than to put too much ink on the rollers and then have to remove it, necessitating a wash-up of the block, too.

The Vandercook 219 press has a motorized inking roller assembly which speeds the distribution of ink. An automatic lock-up bar holds a zinc relief etching in place for Kathy Herbeck of Manhattanville College.

The cylinder and attached inking rollers pass over the block, inking it twice between impressions.

To print a large sheet of paper without slurring or blurring of the edges of the printed matter, it may be necessary to hold the trailing edge of the paper tight against the cylinder as it prints.

Printing from the Columbian or Albion Press

The use of the Albion press has dwindled to a very low point in fine printmaking. It is suitable for small blocks, however, and some wood engravers still find them helpful. The block must be inked with a brayer. Because the edges of the blocks usually print darker, make-ready should be done with care for each block, building up the packing with thin sheets of paper pasted to the packing sheet with Sphinx paste. The make-ready paper should be torn or the edges sanded in order to have a gradual transition in thickness. The block must be placed in the center of the bed of the press; and while the bed is being rolled in and out for alternate inking and printing, care must be taken not to cause bumping or jogging that may loosen the block and cause slurring or blurred prints.

The pressure exerted by one of these old platens is considerable and may easily damage a block if it is excessive. Therefore the pressure should be built up gradually by increasing the number of pieces of paper or cardboard under the block to raise it to proper printing level. Pressure may also be increased by adding to the packing sheets placed between the tympan sheets. These packing sheets cushion the pressure and distribute it somewhat over the surface of the block. A tiny speck of lint or sand can cause pitting or denting of the block in any press, including cylinder and platen presses, and great care must be taken to keep the inking slab and roller clean.

A bookbinding press may be used to print small woodcuts if the edition is limited. The pressure is usually good, but the amount of manipulation is quite time-consuming. Hand rubbing is faster.

Printing from a Low Relief Surface

It is possible to print from a surface where the depth of relief is too low for normal methods, such as with an underbitten relief etching. Instead of inking the plate directly with the roller, which would almost certainly contact the lower areas where they are not deep enough, ink a piece of heavy oak-tag paper evenly and completely. Then place the inked surface on and facing the plate, place a piece of mat board or smooth cardboard on top of that, and, and run it through the etching press with reduced pressure. You will find that only the raised areas will receive the ink. It is possible to use this process without the press by burnishing or spooning the back of the oak tag carefully and with heavy pressure. This will ink the plate, which must now be printed onto your paper either by spooning or by using the etching press. You may use heavy acetate or vinyl instead of tag paper, as it cleans easily and may be reused. The William Blake relief etchings were very shallow and were printed by a similar method.

When the cylinder is run to the foot of the press the paper is placed in position, resting on the slanted paper support. The grippers will pull the paper through the printing cycle.

When the cylinder has returned to the head of the press the grippers release and the printed impression may be checked for flaws.

The Color Relief Print

Color in the woodcut was first used in the West to hand tint the early black and white woodcuts of saints and the designs of woodcut printed playing cards. It was a cheap means to supply colored pictures to the widely illiterate public of the late Middle Ages. The use of color from several wood blocks was introduced in western Europe in the second half of the 15th century for heraldic cuts, initials, and printer's marks. The method of printing pictorial color woodcuts from separate blocks, known as "Chiaroscuro," appeared in 1508 in Germany in the earliest dated print. However, according to Hind, the first of the Italian Chiaroscuro woodcutters, Ugo Da Carpi, about 1455–1523, was no doubt making prints much earlier. These prints, though printed from separate blocks, were tonal and interpreted the line and wash drawings of the period. Da Carpi and other fine woodcutters worked from designs by Parmigiano and Raphael and were essentially reproductive. The emphasis was on various tones of one color but sometimes included browns, yellows, and greens on the same print.

Some woodcuts with color as a unifying structural element were made by the Chinese as early as the 17th century. However, it is the multicolor prints of 18th and 19th century Japan that have given us such an eloquent concept of color in the woodcut. The ukiyo-e prints (the pictures of the Floating World, the World of Everyday Life) were made by major artists with great refinement and taste for the generally poorer classes and the uneducated. They were bought for a few yen, with little value attached to them, much as the medieval woodcuts were purchased in Northern Europe in the 16th century. They were souvenirs, pasted in homes, bought by travelers. The subject matter covered a wide range: girls, actors, genre scenes, popular landscapes. Utamaro, Sharaku, Harunobu, Hokusai, and Hiroshige were among the great names.

There are many tales of the Ukiyo-e prints first arriving in Paris as packing material for art objects. However, as early as 1775 a Swedish naturalist, Carl Peter Thunberg, spent considerable time in Nagasaki and made a collection of Ukiyo-e. Dutch sea captains in the early 1800s formed extensive collections that were known in Paris. In 1860, the British magazine *Once a Week* contained articles of a voyage in Japan illustrated with some of Hiroshige's landscapes. By 1862 a Japanese curio shop opened in Paris and sold many of the Ukiyo-e prints. In 1867 the Paris Exposition Universelle exhibited a large quantity of Ukiyo-e, and the Paris art world became profoundly aware of the new art forms.

Opposite: Kitagawa Utamaro
"The Awabi Fishers" (from a triptych)
Color woodcut 15½" x 10¾"
Collection of the authors

It was from this exhibition that many western artists incorporated the concepts of the Ukiyo-e into their work. Though the art was declining in intensity and quality in Japan, it was a great influence on the creativity of the avant-garde in Paris. Gaugin, Van Gogh, Mary Cassatt, Toulouse-Lautrec, Whistler, Degas, Manet, and Pissarro came under the influence of the asymetric compositions, strong design, and stylized form. The flat color, pattern, and line as intrinsic compositional elements were deeply inspiring to those artists.

Though the early influence of the Japanese print was felt more directly in Western painting, it also rapidly affected the approach to color in printmaking.

Gauguin's use of the woodcut had a strong Japanese influence. His blocks were conceived in black and white, but the use of color in the print interested him. He experimented with printing a block in black, then reinking it in another color, usually brown, and printing it slightly off register. In some prints he added brilliant color through stencils or hand colored the prints. Gauguin's innovative approach with the woodcut influenced the woodcuts of Munch. Gauguin's probes into the use of color in the print no doubt helped Munch to explore the color print even further than Gauguin had taken it. In some instances Munch used separate blocks for each color, in others he used one block cut into separate color areas, inked separately, and reassembled for printing with one rubbing. These are powerful prints, where color and form are synonymous.

Another major innovation occurred with Picasso's linocuts of the 1950s. His use of one block for a multicolor print was probably the first time anyone had devised a reduction method for cutting and printing each color out of one block.

Since the late forties and fifties, color in the relief print has become increasingly adventurous and freewheeling. Michael Rothenstein in England and Carol Summers and Seong Moy in the United States were early experimenters.

The flexibility of the cardboard relief print and the collage print along with inventive ways of inking with small rollers has expanded the use of color. Op and Pop images have also loosened conceptual ideas about color and have helped to break down old taboos about color in the print.

USE OF COLOR

The use of color in the development of the relief-print image should help to clarify the visual idea and express form. Employing color as mere decoration or as a "tint" to a black-and-white print will not normally produce an exciting or satisfying work. If the artist understands and exploits the great potential of color in a relief print a work of high expressive power can be resolved. The woodcut block itself has a quality that makes the colors take on vibrancy and intensity. It is easy to cut separate blocks for each color and to print them in correct register to achieve the final impression of many colors in one image. It is also possible to use a single block to print all the colors in a design. This method, known as the *reduction* or *subtractive* method, was the one used so eloquently by Picasso in his linoleum color prints. This process will be discussed in the section on reduction prints. The procedures an artist uses in the color relief print are extremely personal and are dictated by his own esthetic direction. We will discuss various methods that have been found logical and useful at various times for our own work and for the work of other artists.

Key Block Method

Some artists will cut a block that contains most or all of the dominant design elements. This block is called a *key block*, and it can be proved in a strong color after it is cut. These proofs may serve as trials for color samples that may be painted directly on the proof, using poster color, water color, or ink to develop the color relationships. From these sketches the other blocks may be cut. The drawback of the key-block method occurs when too much emphasis is placed on the first block and the succeeding colors become only incidental to the design rather than essential to it. The Japanese Ukiyo-e prints used a key block with the major elements in black line and the areas of mass and pattern in successive color blocks.

Color on Block Method

Another approach is to develop a color sketch directly on a block, painting the image with poster or tempera paint, using thin pigment so that the grain is not filled with color. After the design is completed, make a careful tracing of it as a record, then cut the most important color on the block. This first block serves as a master that may be proved in register onto the successive blocks. The tracing you have made will enable you to cut the shapes of the next colors. The drawback of this method is that you destroy your color sketch when you cut the first block. However, it eliminates one transfer and keeps the first block very vigorous and fresh, which is a very positive factor.

The Separate Color Sketch

The most complete control is obtained when a carefully worked out color drawing is completed on a separate sheet. This is an excellent means for those who must have a completely realized solution before they start. The sketch should be made in a medium that can reflect the transparencies possible in color overprinting. Watercolor is good, colored inks are better, and poster color or tempera are suitable if used properly. As poster colors are opaque, the basic colors of each block may be mixed in small dishes and used to mix smaller batches of the secondary colors that will be fairly close to the finished print from the blocks.

Pastels may be used for the same result, as may pencil crayons. These are excellent for small-scale work if used on tracing paper. The color range is quite good in the larger artist's sets. Colors may be applied over each other to approximate the quality of overprinted inks. Felt pens, using dyes, are excellent, although they tend to fade after a few months. Colored paper can be used in making a collage sketch to serve as a guide for a color relief print. With any of these methods, a tracing will have to be made of the completed sketch to serve as the master guide for all the blocks to be cut. The results from this method are not likely

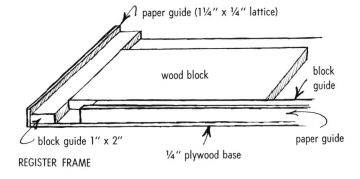

paper guide (1¼" x ¼" lattice)

wood block

block guide

block guide 1" x 2"

¼" plywood base

paper guide

REGISTER FRAME

to be as fresh and spontaneous as with other, more direct approaches. However, the increase in control of color relationships has certain advantages for those artists who desire complex color statements. The choice of method is really directed by the personal direction of each artist, and the success of each procedure depends upon his enthusiasm and drive.

COLOR REGISTRY METHODS

Register Frame

After your preliminary color sketch is completed and your first block is cut, it is necessary to place this first image on each successive block, in proper register or juxtaposition, in order to have each color area in proper relation to the other. A register frame is easily constructed; on a base of ¼" plywood or pressed wood or composition board, nail or glue two pieces of 1" by 2" wood, as shown. These pieces are at right angles to each other and hold the block in place. If you habitually use cardboard or linoleum or other thin blocks you can make the frames from thin stripping. In any case they should approximate the thickness of the blocks that you are printing. Along the edges of this wooden angle nail or glue two strips of thin ⅛" by 1" wooden stripping to serve as a paper guide. Take care to leave an open corner when you fasten the stripping so that the thumb can comfortably adjust the paper. Two wooden 12" rulers make excellent paper guides.

The first block, after it is cut, is inked fairly heavily and placed in the frame. Slide the block against the long edge of the frame until it touches the other, perpendicular side. Make sure that the long edge is firmly fitted in the frame. This position must be duplicated every time the block is printed. If the block is square both edges may fit securely, but it is more likely that the block is slightly out of square and one side fits solidly while the other edge touches at one point only. When the block is in position, tape a piece of tracing paper to the edge of the frame.

Offsetting onto Additional Blocks

Tracing paper is used in preference to all other papers because it is not absorbent and will hold a great deal of ink on its surface in order to offset the cut image onto the other uncut blocks. Let the tracing paper drop down over the well-inked first block. Rub your hand over the back of the paper to hold it firmly. Now rub the back of the tracing paper with a rubbing tool to obtain a strong image on the tracing paper.

Lift up the tracing paper with the imprint of the block on it, being careful not to remove the paper from the frame. Slip out the block that has just been printed. Turn the block over to the uncut side and slip the block back into the register frame carefully in the same position.

Drop the tracing paper onto the block. Rub it with the hand to adhere it and then with a rubbing tool to achieve a strong image on the uncut block. Lift up the tracing paper again, remove the block, and slip in the next uncut block

When printing color blocks, always place the block into the register frame in the same way for each printing to achieve a consistent register, using the block guides.

To transfer a design cut into a block to another block in order to achieve color register, ink the block, then place it in the register frame. Put a piece of nonabsorbent paper (tracing paper or bond paper) in position with masking tape. Rub the paper with the spoon to print the inked design.

Below: Now turn the block over or place a new, uncut block in the register frame, leaving the taped tracing paper in position.

until the first cut image has been successfully transferred, in position, onto each uncut block.

Let the offset images of the first block dry on the uncut color blocks. Wash off the ink from the first cut block with varnolene so that the pores of the wood will not be clogged. After the offset images are dry, the second color can be indicated with chalk or traced on the block from a drawing, in direct relationship to the first color. Care must be taken to make the image of the second color a little larger to allow for an overlap of colors so that no gaps of white paper will appear between forms. This technique is called *trapping* and requires an overlap of $\frac{1}{16}''$ or so. After the second color is cut, the transfer is repeated, placing the image onto tracing paper and then onto the third or fourth blocks that are to be cut. This time, instead of using a dark ink, use a light red or green ink to roll up the second block so that it can be seen clearly in relation to the first color offset.

An aid in using this method is to avoid cutting any of the blocks completely; thus the composition can develop organically, and changes can be easily made after first proofing. When printing an edition from the register frame, the paper should be trimmed in advance to have two straight sides, at right angles to each other. These sides fit into the paper guides on the frame and must always be placed in the same manner, from block to block, in order to maintain the same relationships. The best way to hold the paper is by diagonally opposite corners, which gives you the most control. Slide the paper along the long edge of the paper guide until it hits the side guide. Then lower the paper on to the inked block and print it by rubbing. Once the ink has adhered the paper to the block, it may be moved out of the guides for the printing process. The inking should also be done with the block away from the frame edges in order to keep them clean and to help keep margins clean.

Japanese Method

The Japanese register method requires blocks somewhat larger than the printed area because the register guides are cut into each block. The white margin around your print is established by the register guides. Small right-angled key stops are cut into one corner and one side of the block. They do not have to be cut very deeply, as they must hold only the edge of the paper. About three times the thickness of the paper you are using is enough. See drawing for details. The

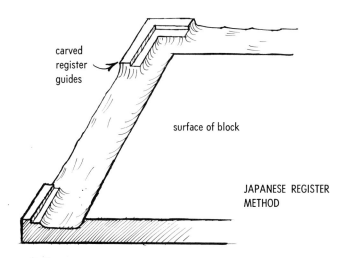

carved register guides

surface of block

JAPANESE REGISTER METHOD

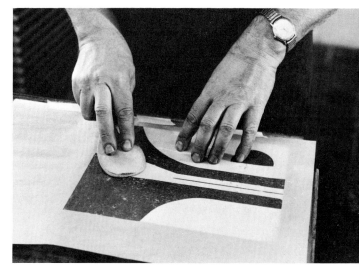

Transfer the wet ink from the tracing paper to the uncut block by rubbing with the spoon. The tape will keep the paper in the correct position.

The design has been transferred, in register, to the new block. This will enable you to see exactly where the first block will fall in relation to the new block.

The paper is placed in position over the inked block, using the paper guides. Use the same placement throughout the edition for consistent register.

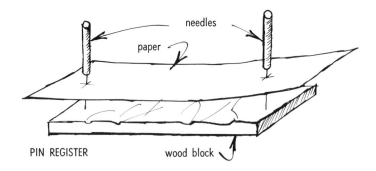

PIN REGISTER

Antonio Frasconi places small blocks on a marked cardboard sheet in order to control their register for a color print. It is not necessary to cut the same size blocks for each color of a color print.

REGISTER FOR THICK RELIEF PRINT OBJECTS

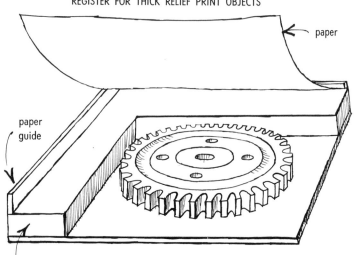

paper is fitted into these stops each time an impression is to be pulled. These registers are cut into each block in succession, as the blocks are cut. The previously cut block is transferred to the uncut blocks either by the Japanese method of gluing the key proof to each block or by the western method of transferring a proof inked on tracing paper or nonabsorbent bond paper by rubbing the back of the proof, while the ink is still wet, on to the next blocks. See the section on the Japanese method. This method restricts the size of the prints, and most western printmakers do not use this technique.

Pin Register

An adequate method for registering small prints uses two long needles. Common pins are usually too small for any but tiny prints. After the first block has been cut, take a heavily inked proof on a strong, tough paper. While the paper is still on the block, punch two needles through the paper into the block. The holes must be close to the edge and far enough apart to insure adequate control. Remove the needles, then the inked proof. Place the proof, image down, on the next block, transfer the image by rubbing the back, punch holes into the new block through the same holes in the paper that you first made. Now cut the second block, and continue this process until all the blocks are cut. When you print using the needle method, you may need help to keep the paper taut and away from the inked surface until the needles have found the holes in the wood. The disadvantages of this method are so great that only small editions may be printed before the process becomes too tedious. Large prints are very difficult to handle, too. The pinholes in the paper are usually easy to burnish closed when the print is dry.

Small Blocks or Pieces

You may need to register a small block or found object into a certain position on a color print. If the block is of thin material, such as cardboard, engraving metal, cloth, or the like, it may simply be glued to a base block of plywood or masonite or chip board. However, if the block is of thicker material, such as 7⁄8″ wood or 3⁄4″ plywood, or cannot easily be glued in place, you can make a base board out of heavy paper or cardboard. Cut this material to the size of the key block or the size of the print. Mark the position of the small block on the base board so that you can return the block to the correct position each time it is inked.

When you are printing from very thick material such as rough-sawn planks or log sections, machine parts, and the like, you may have to make a special jig or frame to hold these pieces in place.

Jigsaw Method

An interesting method of making a color print from one block should be mentioned here because it eliminates registry yet enables the artist to use a multiplicity of color. This approach was used by Edvard Munch, the gifted Norwegian expressionist painter and printmaker who lived from 1863 to 1944. His work with color in the print was unique for his

Edvard Munch
"Two Beings" 1899
Color woodcut, cut block 17" x 23½"
Museum of Modern Art, New York

time. He used it boldly and symbolically in his images. Although he used four or five colors in one print, they were often printed from one block sawed into separate pieces very much like a jigsaw puzzle. After inking each separate piece, he would fit the elements back together again and print the complete image quite easily with one rubbing. *Two Beings* was printed from one block carefully sawn into two separate pieces. The two simple elements, the couple and the ground, and the sky were each cut along the edges of their forms. A thin dividing line appears in the print where a slight space occurs between the forms. This line becomes an integral part of the design and seems to preview the appearance of white separating lines that appear so frequently in contemporary intaglio plates that are cut into separate pieces and inked and reassembled in printing. To produce this effect, mat board or cardboard may be cut into segments, inked separately, and then reassmbled into correct position for printing. Of course, the surface of the mat board should be sealed with lacquer, shellac, or polymer gesso before inking.

Reduction Print

The reduction method is best described by its name. One block is reduced in numerous stages to a multicolored print. It is an interesting and creative procedure for the experienced artist. However, it would be best for the uninitiated to prepare a careful color sketch that will help to clarify the sequential cutting of areas.

The first color is sometimes printed from the whole block. Sometimes a minimal amount of wood is removed to designate the first color. The number of the edition must be determined with the printing of the first color, as there is no possibility of reprinting. After printing the first color, remove all the ink from the block, indicate the second color on the block, and cut away all the excess wood. Ink the block with the second color and print it over the first color. Repeat the cutting and inking until a satisfactory image develops. With this method the area of the block is reduced with each cutting so that the larger areas of color must be cut first. The final block will, of necessity, contain only a small percentage of the area of the block.

Picasso completed a fine series of vibrant color linocuts between 1961 and 1963 that are reduction prints and interesting to study in preparation for using this method.

COLOR INKS FOR RELIEF PRINTING

The chemistry involved in the production of today's printing ink is so complex that a new profession has evolved, that of ink chemist or engineer. Some manufacturers go to great lengths to keep their formulas secret, and the technology of ink manufacture has become so sophisticated that the artist and printmaker should not attempt to make his own color, except in rare cases. It is suggested that you buy ink from a well-establshed commercial firm and conduct a few simple tests of the permanence of some key colors. You will probably find that the great majority of color is relatively permanent and a small number of colors fade quite rapidly and are unsuitable for use.

In general, the earth colors such as the ochres, umbers, and siennas are usually permanent. The cadmiums, yellow, orange, and red, are also permanent in most cases. When you add black, white, transparent extender, and the phthalo blues and greens, you will have a pretty fair palette.

The colors that tend to fade are the reds, magentas, purples, and certain blues. The pigment used in the manufacture of the ink is responsible for the fading in almost every instance. It is usually not specified which pigment has been used in the composition of the ink and it is difficult to predict which exact color is not permanent. When in doubt, roll out a thin film of ink onto a few white matboard cards. Place one in the sun, one in a shady spot, and file another away in an enclosed book or file. After a month or two you will see the amount of fading in each case. Very few colors will pass the sun test without some fading, but all should pass the shade test. Use the best pigments you can get.

As the artist printmaker has a prime interest in the permanence of his colors, he will have to take proper care to guarantee that all his inks are stable. Many artists mix their own colors. They add a good quality oil paint (one without excessive filler, binder, or extender) to a transparent white ink extender in order to get the proper viscosity. Oil paint directly from the tube, although made of high-quality ground

Clare Romano
"Rocks of Truro" 1962
Color woodcut 17½" x 26"
Collection, Brooklyn Museum

pigments, rarely has enough stickiness to roll out properly when inking a relief print. The amount of transparent extender (basically a varnish) will vary according to the viscosity required. In any case, add only the minimum extender needed to achieve good rolling quality. A small amount of dry magnesium can be added to the color to make it stiffer.

It is not so useful to purchase inks in a transparent state, such as transparent lemon yellow, as to buy ink in the opaque state and purchase a separate amount of transparent white. It is not a white pigment at all but a transparent varnish of tannish color that does not alter the intensity of other colors. The transparent white will enable you to control the amount of transparency and to add transparency to any color that you choose. The primary colors, called the process colors by ink manufacturers, will produce a wide range of hues and used with black and white, can extend your palette to a very wide spectrum. However, such colors as emerald green and intense magentas and purples may have to be purchased specially in order to gain maximum brilliance and intensity.

Unless you use ink rapidly, you should buy it in tube form. Many makers put up a good range of color in large tubes (about 1½" in diameter by 7" long). Tube ink is slightly more expensive per pound than ink in cans but is much more convenient to use. We have some tubes of ink that are ten years old and still in good condition. Replace the caps carefully, after cleaning the cap with a rag or palette knife. If you do use canned ink, and it is cheaper, you should wipe the rims and lids and replace the circular waxed paper by smoothing it over the ink in the can, eliminating the air bubbles. When the ink skins over, the top must be scraped off and discarded. Even a small piece of dried ink skin can be an annoyance when printing. Another aid in storing partially used ink cans is to fill the remainder of the can with water to retard the drying-out process. Spray cans of sealers for cans of ink can also be purchased from ink companies and are useful in keeping ink from drying out. A thin film is sprayed over the ink surface.

COLOR PRINTING

Sensitive printing of the color blocks is a vital step in the completion of the final image. A thorough knowledge of the use of overprinting and color sequence can exploit the use of color with variation and inventiveness.

Transparency and Sequence

The use of transparencies in overprinting is an important aspect of the color woodcut. It enables the artist to achieve a wide color range with just a few colors and to use the full potential of the blocks.

Clare Romano
"Summer Garden" 1958
Cardboard relief 18¾" x 24"

A varnish-like material called transparent white is manufactured by many ink makers. When it is added to the color inks it will make them transparent. It is often tannish in color but it does not appreciably alter the color quality of the inks when mixed with them. From 40% to 60% transparency may be added to an ink to achieve the desired quality. The transparency should be added to the ink on the mixing slab and mixed well with a palette knife. The amount of transparency is determined by the color. A lemon yellow or bright orange needs little or no transparency because of the natural transparency of the color itself.

You will find that it is much easier to roll up a block with the color inks because they are of a softer consistency. Less ink is required on the block and less rubbing in printing. If delicate cutting is to be printed, you may find it desirable to add some powdered magnesium to the ink in order to stiffen it.

Generally speaking, the dark colors are printed first and the light ones last in order to achieve the most effect from overprinting with transparent inks. However, there are times when a dark or black block is a key block and it is necessary to the design to print it last.

The color quality of a color print can be greatly changed if the sequence in printing is reversed. Experimentation will lead you to the varied possibilities that exist through sequential printing. Colored papers can also be used with a wide range of effects. Light colors can be printed over black and off-black papers. High-key colored papers and subtle colors can all be used with very surprising qualities.

Wet and Dry Printing

Wet and dry printing is very important in proving. Usually when transparency is used the colors are printed wet over dry or semidry inks. Sometimes when two colors are close in value, even with some transparency added to the second color, they must be printed wet on wet for best transparency results. It is difficult to make firm suggestions in this area. Experimentation with the blocks is of prime importance. So much depends on the color value. Best results can be achieved after a few possibilities are tried.

Exploration of Texture

Interesting color variations can be achieved by overprinting a combination of a smooth block and a textured block or two textured blocks. Flecks of pure color will appear in whatever pattern the textures make.

Use of Small Rollers

There are other possibilities in the printing and the planning of color blocks. Two or three colors can be easily printed on one block if the color is in isolated areas. Small rollers can be used very successfully for these places. There are some small Hunt rollers that come in sizes from 1½" to 6". There are also smaller Craftool rollers of 1" in length and ½" in diameter. All these rollers are quite soft and very good for non-detailed work. If a harder roller is desired, it is best to make one's own. Check sources and methods under section on rollers.

Split Fountain Printing

An interesting way to print more than one color at a time involves a press. A Vandercook, Kelly, or other flat press works very well. The colors are placed on the rollers, not too close together, and the inking rollers are then worked until the ink has been distributed evenly. The colors will merge and blend where they overlap, and this effect can occasionally be used to great advantage. As the ink keeps on blending, there is a limit to the number of prints that can be made before the color is merged or changed. Of course, this effect can be obtained with hand brayers, too, if the length of the roller is long enough to take the blending effect. The method is tricky, however, and can be easily overdone, becoming quite flashy or commercial-looking if not used with discretion.

Carol Summers Method

A unique method of color printing from separate blocks that is worth mentioning has been developed by the New York artist Carol Summers. Summers works with large, simple, stylized or abstracted forms, very often of landscape or architecture. He cuts his blocks fairly deeply, usually of ¼″ plywood. After the blocks are cut he places them in a register frame, lays a piece of woodcut paper down on the uninked block, and rolls a thin film of oil-based ink on the paper with small rollers. Separate blocks are inked in this manner. When all the blocks are printed and the ink is still wet, Summers sprays the whole print with a thin film of varnolene with a mouth atomizer or a spray gun, allowing the colors to run together slightly, giving a watercolor effect to the printed image. Sometimes Summers combines the traditional method of rolling ink on the block with rolling ink on the paper. At times he prints on the back of the print so that the image is diffused. The resulting prints are very handsome and quite similar to rubbings.

JAPANESE WOODCUT METHOD

We have touched on some of the history of the Japanese woodcut, the ukiyo-e, in our introduction to the woodcut. It is not our function to involve ourselves in its rich history in this chapter, but to give some of the basic technical methods that the Japanese have used so eloquently in their prints. It would be well to mention the vast difference in the basic approach to printing the color woodcut in the Japanese Ukiyo-e prints as compared with our contemporary woodcuts that use the woodgrain as an important element and relate the printing to overprinting colors. The use of the water-based inks in the Japanese prints and the application and blending of watercolor washes directly on the blocks enabled them to achieve amazing watercolor qualities and impressions that would seem to us to be closer to monotypes. However, the application was so skilled that the printers were actually able to repeat complicated wash effects and still have consistent multiple editions.

The traditional approach of the Japanese artist to the use of his materials is quite ritualistic. The mastery of manual skill that was demanded of the Ukiyo-e artisans is an impossibility in our culture. However, it is very possible for the contemporary artist to adapt some of the methods for his own expression and with this intent in mind we will try to give some rudimentary information on materials and procedure.

Materials

Wood (cherry, poplar)
A good cutting knife
V gouge
2 sizes of C gouges
Small chisels
Large chisels
Whetstones for sharpening tools
Baren for rubbing
Dosa (sizing for paper made of water, animal glue, and alum)
Animal glue in stick form for making dosa
Alum, 3 to 4 oz. for making dosa
Tube of library paste or rice paste
Pigment
Brushes, large and small horsehair, for applying color
Brush for sizing, called a dosabake
Sumi ink
General equipment for stacking
Paper, boards for cutting, bowls, and the like

Wood

Cherry or yamazakura wood (a species of wild cherry) was almost the only kind of wood used by the traditional ukiyo-e artists. Cherry is a very hard wood and difficult to cut but was very necessary for the fine lines and great detail so prevalent in the ukiyo-e prints, as well as the common large editions.

The traditional ukiyo-e blocks were always cut with the grain. The selection of wood was a very important aspect of the preparation of the block. The wood was most often cut from the central portion of the tree between the heart and the bark, and a regular grain was preferred. The blocks were allowed to season for a few years to make them quite dry, as it is important in working with water-based pigments that the blocks absorb some of the color during printing.

The contemporary Japanese artist is very likely to use any wood that relates to what he wishes to say. Bass plywood is one of the woods most commonly used. It is inexpensive and easy to cut and comes in large sizes. Its unobtrusive grain also makes it desirable. American plywoods such as birch and fir are available and can be successfully used. Birch plywood in ¼″ and ½″ thicknesses, imported from Finland by Stewart Industries in Chicago and listed under our source list, is ideally suited for the woodcut in general and for the Japanese method in particular and is quite inexpensive. In addition to plywood, boards of pine, poplar, or fir can be used.

Tools (For Cutting)

The tools used by the Japanese are few and simple. They do not differ much from the ones suggested in our section

Mallet, chisels, and gouges used by Ansei Uchima in cutting his blocks (frequently made of birch plywood).

Uchima sharpens his tools on a smooth Japanese whetstone *(toishi)*, using water as a lubricant.

Two barens, the one on the right with a split in its bamboo sheath cover, which will be replaced.

Below: The baren taken apart: on the left the old cover about to be replaced, at the top center the coil bamboo cord. At the bottom center is the backing paper that gives the baren its circular shape. The piece of bamboo sheath on the right will be shaped and trimmed to form a new cover for the baren.

on the western manner of the woodcut, but we do list the traditional ones here and suggest that they be used as described in that section. Their use by the ukiyo-e artisans was ritualistic. Certain tools were used only for certain kinds of cutting. The cutters themselves were divided into very distinct areas of work. There were separate cutters for figure work. The highly skilled workers cut the heads and the fine lines of the features and hair. Other cutters worked on the bodies and the pattern of drapery. Less experienced cutters worked on color blocks or unimportant areas. Their training took as long as ten years, and only a few achieved the skill necessary to work on the delicate faces, hair, and hands.

A good knife is essential for cutting lines. It is one of the most important tools. Tiny areas can be cleared with assorted small knives.

Chisels in small sizes are used for cutting out small areas of wood. The larger broad chisels are used for cleaning out large areas and for making *kento* (registry) cuts on the blocks. Sometimes a wooden mallet is used to hit the back of the chisel in order to clear areas in hardwood blocks.

The V gouge and C gouges were not used by the ukiyo-e artists but can be useful additional tools to define forms and to clear small areas.

Whetstones

Whetstones have traditionally been used by ukiyo-e artisans for sharpening tools. They are available in rough, medium, and smooth surfaces and are used with water for sharpening the tools. The stones used extensively by western printmakers use oil as a lubricant.

The edge of the knife or the gouge or chisel is held parallel to the surface of the whetstone. Water is applied so that the stone's surface is always wet. Use a smooth whetstone to finish off the sharpening. Do not change the angle of the tool during sharpening or the edge will be uneven.

The V gouges or C gouges can be sharpened on whetstones with grooves to hold variously sized tools. They can also be sharpened on a flat whetstone, but care must be taken to keep the edge of the curve flush with the stone's surface and to rotate it evenly to keep the edge and the curve at the same time.

Baren

The baren is the pressing and rubbing tool used for printing. It is an ingenious, simple tool that is beautifully designed for use on the porous Japanese paper. It consists of flat, coiled cord strands, strips of bamboo sheath, and a backing disk. The backing disk, about 5½″ in diameter, is made of many layers of Japanese paper, molded on a form, covered with silk tissue, and lacquered. The backing disk holds the coil of cord, and the bamboo sheath used as a covering and as a rubbing surface on one side is twisted into a secure handle on the other side.

Barens come in different weights depending on the thickness of the cord used. The thicker it is, the stronger the pressure it can exert in printing. Only a few traditional printer-artisans can make a proper baren; however, all the Japanese artists cover their own barens. The inside of the baren lasts for years and can be recoiled. The bamboo sheath covering must be replaced often because of the constant rubbing. For the western artist who is not ready to cover or make his own baren, adequate ones are available in art supply stores. The baren can be used for some printing of oil-based inks when the print does not require too much pressure. It works best when used for water-based pigments.

The fine brushes on the left are used for applying the water color to the block in the Japanese method. The coarse brush at right serves to mix the rice paste into the water color prior to its application to the block.

Pigment

At the core of the difference between the Japanese method and the western method is the use of water-based pigment by the Japanese and oil-based inks by western artists.

A variety of kinds of water-soluble paints must be experimented with before the artist can decide which will best express his image.

In choosing a black, you will find quite a difference in printing quality between sumi black, watercolor black, gouache, or poster black. The sumi ink is more of a dye and really penetrates the paper. Water color is a bit more uneven but does penetrate the paper too. Gouache penetrates less but prints strongly, and its colors are of excellent quality and not fugitive. Poster color can print unevenly with some of the color penetrating and some lying on the surface.

Any good quality tempera or water color such as Windsor Newton or Grumbacher will work well.

Brushes for Applying Pigment

Brushes instead of rollers are used for applying pigment to the block. Two types of brushes are used, one for applying pigment over large areas and one for small areas. These brushes are also used for blending and grading color. The brushes are made of horsehair and wood or bamboo. Most Japanese artists soften the hairs of their brushes by rubbing the hair against a piece of sharkskin with a little water for a half hour or more to soften the ends and split the hair tips. Care must be taken to wash the pigment out of the brushes.

Larger water color brushes (called *enogu-bake*) for putting the color on the block. All the brushes and tools shown are used by Ansei Uchima.

These wide flat brushes are *mizubake* and are used for applying water or sizing to the sheet of paper.

Below: The ends of the hairs in the brushes are split and softened by rubbing them against a piece of sharkskin nailed to a board.

Paper

The choice of paper for the Japanese method is in many ways more important than when oil-based inks are used. The degree of absorbency of the paper is important in relation to the kind of effect desired in the image. The strength of the size used on the paper can be a controlling factor in absorbency. Hosho, Torinoko, and Masa papers are all easily available in this country and produce good results. Hosho has especially fine qualities for water-based printing. It is absorbent, yet strong, and allows the printer to rub it extensively without tearing. Because it is so tough, it also seems immune to shrinkage and expansion, a very useful characteristic in the Japanese method.

Sizing

Presized paper is available with one or two sides sized from Nelson Whitehead, Aiko, or direct from Japan. Kizuki-Bosho, the paper used by Ansei Uchima, is sized on both sides and is made by a Tokyo papermaker whose family has

been making paper for seven generations. The name and address of the firm appears in the listing of paper houses in the back of the book.

If an artist wishes to exploit the sensitivity of the relation of the pigment to different kinds of sizing, it is well for the artist to have some knowledge of sizing techniques.

The Japanese name for the size is Dosa. It is prepared by boiling dry animal glue in stick form in water in a double boiler and adding alum to the glue and water after the glue is dissolved. The relative amounts should be:

> 1 gallon water
> 8 oz. glue (animal glue in stick form)
> 3 to 4 oz. alum

Preparation

1. Place the water in a pan or double boiler large enough to take the dipping of the 10″-long brush for applying the size.
2. Break the stick glue into pieces and place it in the water.
3. When the glue is softened a bit, place the pan on medium heat and stir it constantly with a wooden stick or spoon. Heat it slowly until the glue is melted.
4. Add the alum and mix very well.
5. Strain the size through some cheesecloth to filter out extraneous particles.

Application

Use a broad, flat brush called a *dosabake* in Japanese. Apply the size while it is hot.

1. Lay paper flat on a large drawing board or wooden table top.
2. Dip the brush in the size and allow it to absorb enough liquid.
3. Draw the brush across the paper one stroke at a time. Start at one end quite vigorously and slow the movement towards the edge to allow uniform coverage.
4. Hang the paper with clips on a line to dry.
5. After one side is dry or semidry, repeat the process on the other side.

Work Setup

The Japanese artist organizes his work setup in a very traditional manner. It is a very logical arrangement and works very well. We recommend that those artists seriously interested in this method use it entirely or adapt some aspects of it.

There are usually four pieces of equipment; a *small chest of drawers* to hold pigment and brushes, a *printing bench* to hold the blocks, a *box with a shelf* to hold dampened paper, and a *flat board* to hold paper after printing (which should be twice the size of the paper). Additional equipment should include brushes for applying pigment, bowl for water used to dilute pigment or to moisten paper, a paste container, and an oil container for camellia oil or baby oil, which is applied to the baren to help it move freely. Most of this equipment has been tested for centuries and is very useful. The Japanese artist sits crosslegged on the floor in front of his setup. If this is uncomfortable for the western artist with different seating habits, the equipment could be arranged on a table for greater comfort.

Preparation of the Drawing

The ukiyo-e artist did not cut his own blocks. Therefore, the drawing for the cutter had to be a very accurate and finished piece of work. The artist would make a line drawing of the image. If it was to be a color print, the key block would be cut first. The drawing was made with sumi ink on thin paper. Today's artist using this method can find the necessary qualities in a paper called minogami. The paper should be sized with dosa and rubbed with a baren to flatten it and to keep it from wrinkling when it is pasted on the block. The sumi ink is still the best ink to use for drawing on the paper. Pen or brush can be used, but do not use ordinary ink because it blurs when the paper is pasted on the block.

Pasting the Drawing on the Block

The pasting of the drawing on the block takes much skill. The paper is thin and soft, and when it absorbs the paste it is quite difficult to manipulate. Try to work according to the following steps:

1. Apply ordinary library paste evenly to the block with the palm of the hand. Roughen the surface a little to produce a slight texture that will make it easier to position the paper on the block.

2. Let the paper fall lightly on the block, in such a way that the drawing side falls on the block and the paper can be maneuvered into proper position quickly before it sticks. Because the drawing is face down on the block it will print as it was drawn and there will be no reversal of image.

3. Rub the middle section softly to fix the position. Hold the left edge with the left hand and rub the paper up and down with the right hand from the right edge to the left edge.

4. Continue rubbing the paper until it sticks firmly.

5. When the paper is half dry, rub the top layer of the paper away with your fingertips until little rolls of paper wear away and the drawing on the lower layer appears clearly visible. The paper will be a thin film, and the drawing will look as if it had been made on the block.

6. The block is now ready for cutting, after it is dry.

Moistening Paper

The paper should be moistened an hour or two before printing to absorb the water uniformly. Use the long flat brush called the *mizubake* or a spray gun to apply water to every other sheet. Pile them neatly and place a board with a weight on it on top to keep the sheets flat.

After about two hours, the sheets can be arranged on the board used for arranging the paper. Lay the first sheet at the left side of the board and place each successive sheet so that its left edge lies about one inch to the right of the left edge of the preceding sheet until the right edge of the board is reached. Lay the next sheet at the left edge and repeat the procedure until all the paper is arranged. Lay a thick sheet of paper across the top of the pile. Additional water can be applied to the top piece of paper with the mizubake brush.

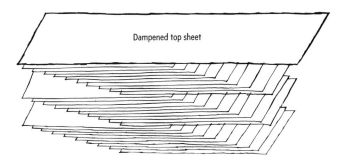

HOW TO DAMPEN JAPANESE PAPER IN STACKS

Cover the stack with a piece of wet cotton fabric and leave overnight.

You will soon know how to judge the proper amount of moisture in the paper after a little experience. Dry weather and humid weather affect the paper and must be taken into consideration. As necessary either add more water or place newsprint paper between every two sheets. If margins become too dry during printing, they must be moistened. If printing must be suspended for any reason, care must be taken to cover the paper with thick wet paper and wet cotton fabric.

Applying Pigment

Pigment is placed on the block with a small bamboo brush. A small quantity of paste is placed on the block, and pigment and paste are mixed and spread over the block with the horsehair applicator brush, adding a few drops of water if necessary. Mix only pigment and paste on the block. Allow the brush to become saturated with pigment and move it in every direction on the block. First use a circular motion to insure mixing the paste and the pigment. Next, use a straight motion across the grain to make the application uniform.

For gradations, rub the block with a wet rag in the area where a fading quality is desired. Dip only one side of the brush in the pigment and rub the brush back and forth over the block a few times to produce a graded tone from the wetness of the block and the pigment.

Use of Baren

Use four fingers to grip the handle of the baren, with the thumb over the handle. Pressure on the baren should be exerted from the palm of the hand so that the force of the rubbing is not just from the wrist but from the whole arm. Stroke the back of the sheet lightly with the baren moving in a circular motion to secure the paper on the block. Next dip a cotton-tipped stick into the camellia oil and dab it over the bottom of the baren. Before each printing rub the baren on a cotton cloth to remove any excess oil

Try to use the weight of the whole body in the rubbing. Start from the righthand corner nearest the printer and continue in a zigzag motion moving forward. When the top of the sheet is reached, start at the bottom again, until the whole sheet is rubbed. Use the baren in short strokes. Proper printing quality is achieved when the pigment penetrates about one half the thickness of the paper. Before removing the paper, rub the edges well and across the grain to be sure the image is uniform.

Remove the print carefully with the left hand from the right corner. Place it carefully on the paper board and examine it for printing quality and color relationships.

Toshi Yoshida, in a demonstration in Provincetown, Mass., applies water color to a cherry wood block with an *enogu-bake* or color brush.

The paper is placed on the freshly inked block and then is rubbed with the baren by Yoshida to make the impression.

Wood Engraving

HISTORY

The history of wood engraving should not be separated from that of the woodcut, as wood engraving was an 18th-century offshoot of woodcutting. However, for our purposes, it is simpler to present the history of wood engraving as an introduction to the section discussing its technique.

Until the 18th century, woodcut images had always been cut into wooden boards, vertical length cut from a variety of medium soft to hard grain trees, from poplar to cherry. Thomas Bewick, the 18th-century English engraver, is often given credit for first using the end grain of the wood. He cut his images in white lines directly into the wood with gravers, instead of knives and gouges and printed from the relief surface of the block. In the woodcut, the image was developed through an intricate pattern of black lines as the positive image, and white negatives areas were removed with gouges as in Durer's woodcuts. There is no doubt that other artist craftsmen experimented with this wood engraving method before Bewick gained fame for his outstanding book illustrations. However, he used the method so extensively and developed it with such skill and sensitivity that there are no contenders for his position as innovator. Its possibilities for detail and tonality soon made it the most popular and practical method to produce illustrations in great numbers for books, magazines and newspapers. The durability of the wood engraving, due to the close grain of the end grain of such hard woods as boxwood and maple, allowed enormous numbers of impressions from one block. A copperplate engraving of the day would begin to break down after fewer prints. One of Bewick's blocks, an illustration for a Newcastle newspaper, produced an edition of 900,000 prints without wearing down. Another great advantage was the ease of locking up the wood engraving and the type in one unit and printing it in one operation.

The application of wood engraving for a growing printing industry hungry for illustrations soon proved to be destructive to original creative expression. Numerous craftsmen of unbelievable skill worked to reproduce drawings and to interpret paintings for mass consumption through wood engravings. Scores of volumes of classics illustrated with Gustav Dore's wood engravings and cut by highly skilled craftsmen had a ready market among a rising middle-class audience. The craft flourished as a purely reproductive process until the late 19th century when photoengraving began to replace the use of the engraved block.

Creative wood engraving was revived in the 20th century through the use of the medium by imaginative book illustrators in England, Germany, and the United States, with notable contributions by Fritz Eichenberg and Lynd Ward in the United States.

It was not until the late 1940s and early 1950s that innovating concepts began to be explored by the American artists Misch Kohn, Leonard Baskin, and Arthur Deshaies (Deshaies working with lucite engraving). Their use of large-

"There are no formulas which can describe an artist's relationship to his work and material—it differs widely with his philosophy, and temperament and character. My own approach to the woodblock is not a purely mechanical or technical one, it is intimate, highly personal, emotional and sensual.

"The first cut made into the darkened surface of a woodblock, with the point of a steel blade or a burin, releases hidden forces which one can hardly gauge beforehand. The steel locates a spark, a source of light spreading slowly over the face of the block as the design emerges, white against black.

"This to me constitutes the never ending excitement—the suspense, the challenge, the surprise, as the graver and the wood take over, guide your eye and hand, create drama in a wealth of light, shadows and textures.

"Metal, linoleum as synthetic surfaces would never do for me what the living wood can do—each block, with its own inherent character, quality of age and grain, and often with its imperfections, offering a new and different challenge.

"Of all the species I have tried, end grain boxwood, slowly aged and cured, carefully planed and polished, has been the best partner in the game. First it was the famous Turkish boxwood, later Cuban and other Latin-American substitutes, less and less durable and reliable as time went on. Endgrain maple, even side grain Swiss pear and cherry had to fill the gap.

"As for the tools, most of them have remained the same old faithful companions over half a century, given to me as a student in Leipzig, often passed on to my own students later—indestructable if treated with due respect, kept razor sharp on an old Arkansas oil stone. Often an electric drill with a flexible shaft is used for grainy textures or for clearing larger areas.

"Not much else is needed except some stiff black ink, some sympathetic Japanese vellum, and some spoon like thing to rub its back with—gently— and a print is born. That—and good light, good eyes, good music—and a lot of patience."

—*Fritz Eichenberg*

Opposite:
Fritz Eichenberg
"The Folly of War" 1971
Woodengraving 18" x 11⅞"
Aquarius Press, Baltimore

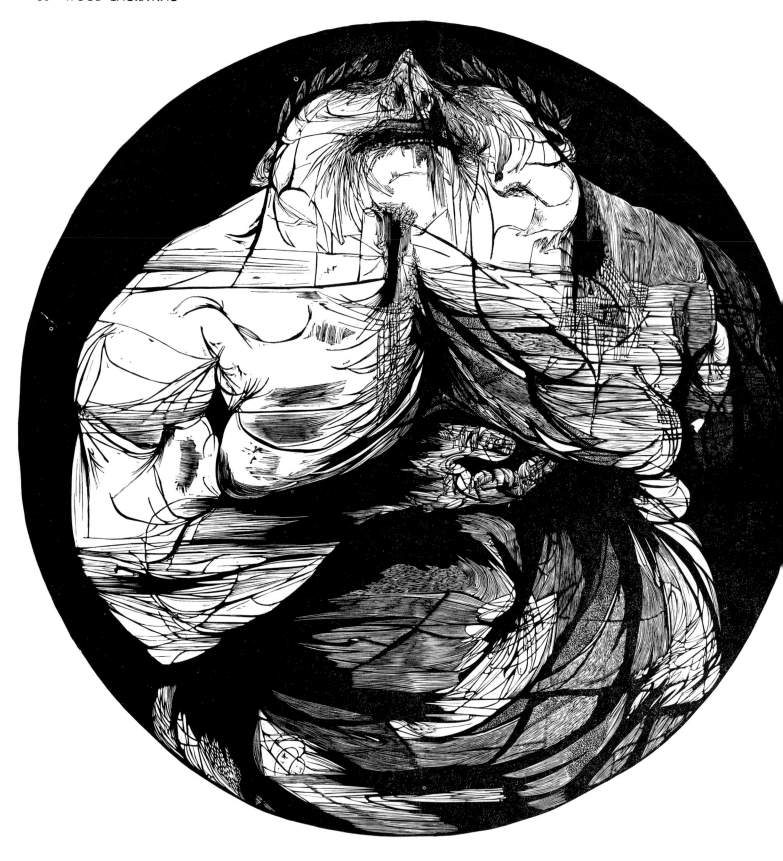

Leonard Baskin
"Death of the Laureate"
Wood engraving 11½" diameter
Collection Ben Sackheim

scale blocks and a freer handling of tools helped to reinstate wood engraving as a medium that complimented contemporary images.

The technique of wood engraving is both demanding and rewarding. The care and patience necessary to plan, cut, and print a wood engraving have deterred many artists from working with this method, but it has attracted a small group of artists who have produced prints of great precision and fine detail and controlled textures. Inevitably, the photo-engraved line cut and half-tone supplanted the wood engraving, and today there are virtually no skilled wood engravers working at their trade.

WOOD

Turkish boxwood, the most desired of all woods, is now very hard to get and quite expensive when available It is usually found as a veneered block, with the top layer of Turkish boxwood and the bottom section of another wood. The next most sought-after wood is South American boxwood, which is about one-half the price of the Turkish variety. Even cheaper is domestic maple, which is one-half the price of the South American boxwood. All these woods are suitable for engraving. The blocks must be made by specialists with precise planing and finishing machinery; because of the many small pieces used to assemble a larger block, the gluing and fitting is a critical operation. Only a few manufacturers remain who still produce blocks of good quality.

DRAWING ON THE BLOCK

All the detail and texture which you desire in your final print must be cut in the block by you. The block offers none of the wood grain, saw marks, or knotholes commonly found in plank grain woodcuts. The wood engraving is done on the end grain of the wood, which offers no variation in resistance to the tools used by the artist.

In general, it is easier to make white lines into a black background than to cut around a black shape on a white background. This simple fact, as true for a woodcut as for a wood-engraving, should be remembered as you prepare your design. The variety of stipples, tones, tints, and textures depends upon the ingenuity of the engraver, but tones based upon white cuts are easier to make than those built up of black lines or dots. If you need cross-hatching, you will find that white line cross-hatching is simple but black line cross-hatching requires cutting out tiny white squares between the lines, a tedious procedure at best.

You may draw directly on the block with pencil or ink to establish the basic areas of the design prior to cutting. If you use pencil, it should not be so hard that it indents the block. These indentations will print as white lines and can ruin a block. Fix the pencil drawing with any good charcoal or pastel fixative so that it doesn't rub off as you work. You can transfer a drawing by using carbon paper If you blacken your block with India ink before you begin it will be necessary to use light colored pencils or white charcoal to transfer

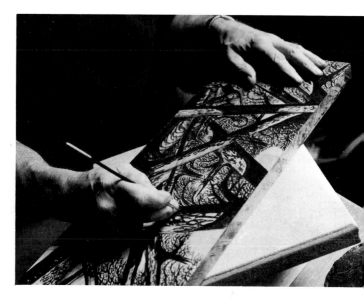

Lynd Ward paints his design directly on an end grain block with india ink in preparation for a wood engraving.

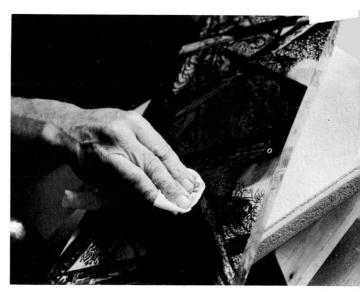

When the india ink has dried Lynd Ward tints the block with red oil color. This will enable him to see exactly where his cut is going.

Lynd Ward
"Pathfinder" 1971
Wood engraving 8" x 22"
Courtesy of the artist

Simplest possible use of capacities of the end grain block using a minimum of engraving tools—only five or six involved.

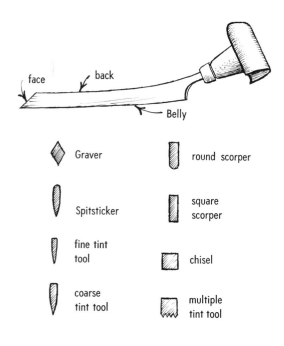

WOODENGRAVING TOOLS

your design onto the block. This method allows you to visualize your final result much better than working on the natural color of the wood. Too much fixative swallows up the tracing, however, and a good compromise is to tint the block with a grey or colored ink, then use black pencil or charcoal to outline the design. When this is fixed it will remain visible. If a felt pen is used, fixative will not be necessary.

Do not work out your preliminary sketch so completely that cutting it becomes a mere tracing of your design. Instead, keep your sketch as an indication of what you want and put your effort into the cutting itself, so that it will be fresh and spontaneous. It is important to keep your enthusiasm strong, and repeated tracings and redrawings of a design are boring and tiring. Besides, the textures and tonalities of the wood engraving are difficult to approximate in a sketch, and it is worthless to spend hours indicating something that you can do better by cutting into the wood.

WOOD ENGRAVING TOOLS

The tools used in engraving lines are called gravers or spit stickers, and tools called tint tools are used when tones are built up. The diagram shows a tool and its parts. The spit stickers are normally used for curved lines, but gravers may also be used to cut curves. When you clear out large areas of white, the scorpers or chisels are used in the same way gouges are used for wood-cuts.

To hold the wood-engraving tool, pick it up from the table as shown in the photo. The thumb guides the tool as it is

The engraving tool is held like this, with the thumb along the shaft of the tool.

In order to turn the block easily Lynd Ward has constructed a rotating turntable that swivels at a touch.

being pushed by the palm of the hand. When curves are being cut, the wood is turned, not the tool. To facilitate the turning of the block, a leather sandbag has traditionally been used as a base for the block, although many substitutes can be devised The sandbag is the most efficient support for smooth turning when cutting precise curves, and anyone who wants to do much engraving will find it a worthwhile acquisition.

A large magnifying glass is very helpful when detailed cutting is necessary. The glass should be mounted on a stand in order to free the hands for work.

The curved belly of the engraving tool serves the purpose of keeping the tool away from the block while the line is being cut. If the tool were straight, the belly of the tool would dent the wood at the beginning of the stroke.

When cutting white areas with the scorpers or gouges, be careful to remove the shoulder of wood that is left after the outline has been cut. This edge doesn't show until the block is being printed, and if printed must be cleared away afterward. Use a thin card to protect the edges when you are gouging out white areas. If you do dent the edges of a black area with the belly of the tool, sprinkle a few drops of water on the dented spot. Light a match and hold the block over the flame so that the water steams and the wood is expanded back to its original shape. Minor dents can be removed in this way, but deep bruises are another matter and require plugging.

PRINTING

The technique of printing a wood engraving is similar in principle to that of woodcut printing, but the ink used should be very stiff and the paper should be smooth and fine. Thin, runny ink will clog or fill the fine textures and tiny stipple openings. The roller used should be gelatine or plastic, in perfect condition, and the ink film must be thin and even.

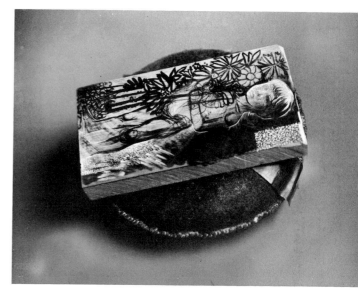

The conventional sandbag is shown here, with a partially cut block, which can turn and tilt as needed. This sandbag is made of felt.

The tool is pushed through the wood, while the block is turned into the cut.

Left: Lynd Ward's press, based on the Washington press, common equipment in the U. S. in the 19th century.

Below: A thin film of stiff ink is rolled over the block with a good roller. An even coat of ink is essential for a fine proof.

The inked block is centered on the bed of the press by Lynd Ward.

The paper is eased onto the block with the assistance of a piece of cardboard. The thin paper tends to sag and the cardboard prevents premature contact with the inked surface.

The lever exerts a downward pressure on the form; because the entire surface is printed at once, great pressure is needed.

Below: When the packing sheets are lifted, the ink shows through the thin paper.

Ink should be thoroughly distributed on the roller. When printing with a burnisher, rub carefully over the entire surface of the paper, using even, steady pressure to eliminate streaks and light spots. There must be enough black area for the ink to act as an adhesive and grip the paper, keeping it from slipping. If your block has too much white area and only a small percentage of black line, it may be necessary to print the block in a press. See the previous section on press printing woodcuts for details.

PAPERS FOR WOOD ENGRAVING

The rough, hand-made papers are rarely suited for wood engravings, and then only when the blocks are press-printed. The best prints are taken on smooth, fine paper, such as India paper and thin Japan paper. The machine-made papers that are smooth and soft will yield better results than heavy, hard papers. It may be necessary to dampen some papers, but they should be damp only, not soaked, as some papers disintegrate when too wet. If you print on a damp sheet by hand burnishing, use a dry piece of paper between the burnisher and the damp sheet as a buffer sheet.

Finishing touches are added with hand burnishing. Lynd Ward protects the thin paper with a card and uses a Japanese bamboo rice spoon as a rubbing tool.

Below: The proof is pulled from the block. The piece of wood in front of the block serves as a guide for the paper in order to keep margins consistent.

Contemporary Relief Methods

THE LUCITE PRINT

The search for new materials to help express the ever-expanding range of esthetic freedom has been a natural outgrowth of the changing image of the print in the last ten or fifteen years. A logical and exciting development has been the artist's awareness of the potential of new materials, developed primarily for industry, that could be used for his own creative use.

Lucite is a material that has been used very individually by a number of artists. Arthur Deshaies, an American printmaker, was one of the first American artists to use the material expansively. He used it for relief engraving and intaglio.

Jack Sonenberg
"Dimensions, 1970 No. 1"
Relief Print, with thread 25" x 21"
Associated American Artists Gallery

The plates are made of newsboard, and covered with an acrylic medium to stiffen them and isolate them from inks and solvents. They will stand up to the printing of large editions. One set of plates is used for color that is rolled onto the surface. All the color is usually printed in one run through the etching press. Another plate is used for blotting ink off the paper, and embossing the paper at the same time. The tonality of the color depends on the different levels in the second plate, and the adjustment of pressure on the press.

It can be cut with engraving tools or the same gouges used for woodcuts. However, the density and hardness of lucite makes it far more resistant than wood. One of the great assets of the material is that it can be purchased in dimensions up to 28″ by 36″, which makes it a highly desirable substitute for the boxwood used in wood engraving, whose largest dimensions are seldom more than 12″ by 20″, because larger sizes would be in danger of breaking. There can be a great deal of freedom in the preparation of the image because the lucite is transparent. A preparatory drawing can be placed under the lucite sheet and used as a clear guide for the artist's cutting.

If a thin film of water-based ink is rolled on the surface and allowed to dry, it will aid the cutting because every cut mark will be clearly visible. Water-based ink is suggested because it can be washed off easily and will leave the surface in its natural state. Tools must be kept very sharp when working the lucite because of the toughness of the material. You must also be careful not to scratch or mar the surface in areas you wish to keep uncut. Lucite is a very sensitive material and responds to the slightest scratches from any sharp tool. A needle or a razor blade can develop interesting areas of texture. An electric drill, a vibro-graver, or any electric tool of this type can be used with great success. The transparency of lucite can also be an assist when the plate is being inked if it is held up to the light to check the build-up of ink before printing a first proof.

The possibilities for drypoint and intaglio printing are many and are discussed under the section on intaglio.

The use of lucite for color printing has distinct advantages. Because lucite is transparent, it is naturally easy to register and to align plates one over the other to check accuracy.

THE CELLOCUT

The cellocut process was developed by Boris Margo, painter, printmaker, and sculptor. It is basically the utilization of a liquid plastic material consisting of sheet celluloid dissolved in acetone.

Solutions of varying consistencies are used to coat any smooth surface such as Masonite, Presdwood, copper, brass, aluminum, or zinc plates. After the liquid has set, it may be worked with etching or woodcut tools. A thicker solution may be applied to form a heavier raised surface. The plates may be printed in relief or intaglio, by hand or with an etching press.

Margo's earliest experiments evolved out of his work with drypoint on celluloid. In the thirties he began to experiment with the celluloid in liquid form and to build up areas with thicker plastic, impressing textures or imbedding materials into the plate itself. Rollers of different degrees of softness and hardness such as gelatine and hard rubber were used in color printing in order to reach recessed and raised surfaces with a wide range of colors.

Boris Margo's inventive work with this medium was a forerunner of the use of collage, assemblage, and acrylic adhesives that took the form of the collagraph in the late fifties and sixties.

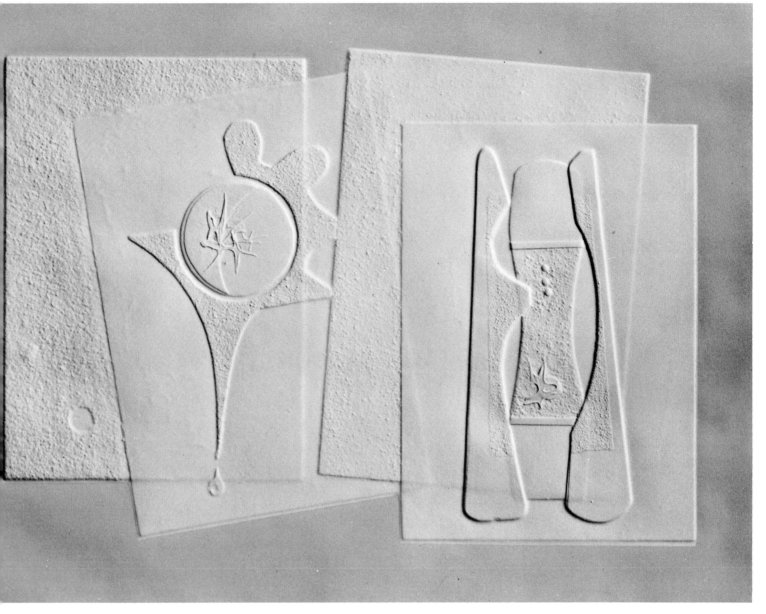

Boris Margo
"Pages from the Book" 1969
Cellocut 20" x 28"
Courtesy of the Artist
Photograph by Arthur Swoger

LINOCUT

The use of linoleum as a craft material and as a means of introducing young children to the print often makes serious artists avoid it. This is unfortunate. Because a material is simple, easily obtained, and easy to cut does not mean that it cannot offer some rather good features. Some excellent work has been done with linoleum by major artists. Matisse and Picasso have used it to great advantage. Matisse was able to produce a sensitive bold line of great fluidity in his *Seated Nude.* Picasso used linoleum for his important series of color reduction prints discussed in the section on that method.

Within the limitations of the medium lie some of its assets. It is very available and therefore inexpensive. The ordinary heavy linoleum of good quality, with canvas backing, is best. It can be purchased in floor-covering stores. Avoid the inlaid or patterned types. A white, light grey, or tan is easiest to use because preparatory drawing with India ink or magic markers is so visible. Prepared blocks can be purchased in art supply stores, but they are much more expensive and their only advantage is that they are mounted on plywood. Mounting on plywood can be done without difficulty

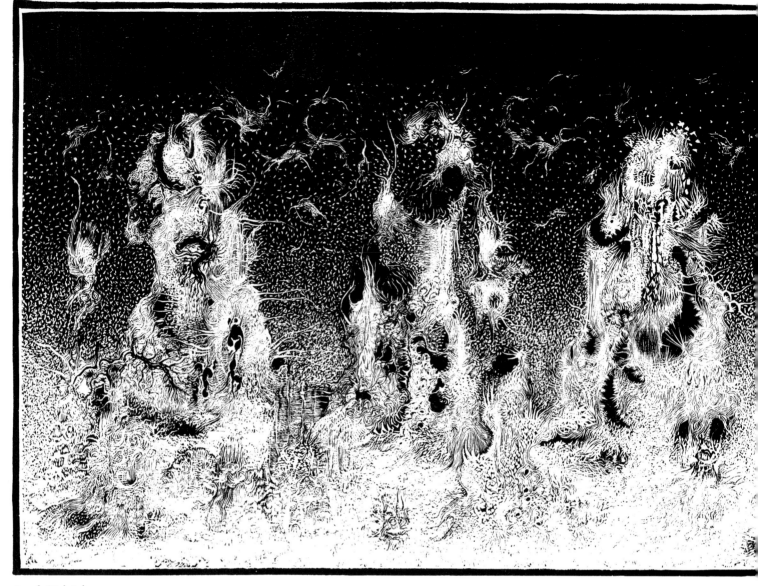

Josef Gielniak
"Improvisation II (Fantaisie sur un theme morbide)" 1959
Linocut 7¹⁄₁₆" x 9⅝"
Pratt Graphics Center

if a wood backing is desired. For a large block this might be an advantage. However, if the printing of a linoleum plate is to be exploited by using an etching press, it is best to leave it unmounted. Detailed discussion of these possibilities are included in the intaglio section. The cutting tools used for linoleum can be the same ones used for the woodcut. They must be kept very sharp, although the material is fairly soft and offers little resistance to cutting. However, there is an abrasive material in linoleum that is very destructive to the cutting edge of your tools. You must sharpen your tools frequently. One of the cutting advantages is that linoleum can be cut in any direction without resistance and is sensitive to punctures and scratches so that textural surfaces can be imposed into it. One method of utilizing interesting textures is to place textured material of not too much height such as sand, wire, metal washers, watch parts, and the like on the linoleum, place a piece of smooth cardboard on top of the objects, and run it through an etching press. The impressions of the objects on the linoleum will be sharp and clear.

Though linoleum imposes little of itself as a material, it serves as an easy vehicle for color. The slightly pebbly quality of its surface can lend a very subtle texture.

Printing the Linocut

The linoleum block is printed exactly the same as the woodcut. The use of rollers and the hand rubbing are no different. However, there is more of an advantage in press printing the linoleum relief than in the woodcut. Because the unmounted linoleum is thin and flat, it can be printed in any etching press. Its relief surfaces can be rolled with ink, the paper placed in position, and a light blanket placed over it. It may then be printed with medium pressure in any etching press.

Etching Linoleum

Linoleum may be etched with caustic soda (sodium hydroxide) and printed as either a relief print or an intaglio print. Various resists, such as etching ground, asphaltum, heated paraffin wax or varnish, may be painted on the block and later scratched or incised into. The caustic soda should be used in a saturated solution and, as it is very dangerous, must be handled with care. It can be brushed or swabbed on the linoleum and replenished as it loses its strength. Deep biting takes hours, unfortunately, and this disadvantage is a serious handicap. Sheet linoleum is becoming hard to find in the United States because of the prevalence of the modular squares now in favor for floor coverings.

HAND EMBOSSING THE RELIEF PRINT

Though it may seem that the inkless embossed print or the color and black and white print with areas of embossing is a very contemporary innovation, embossing was used by the Japanese for whole areas of pattern in prints as early as the 18th century. This method was called *gauffrage*. Hand embossing a relief print is done by forcing dampened thick Japanese rice paper into the recessions or cut-away areas in a woodcut, linoleum cut, or any relief print. The areas that are embossed are the negative white areas. It is said that Okumura Masanobu was the first of the ukiyo-e artists to use embossing. Some artists used it to define pattern in garments, and sometimes an object such as a scroll or a headress was embossed. Utamaro used embossing in some of the women's faces of his prints. Harunobu, Buncho and Shunsho also made effective use of embossed areas in their prints. Crude use of embossing was made in England in the early 18th century by J. B. Jackson. French artists in the late 19th century experimented with inkless embossings much like our cast paper prints.

High-relief embossing can be achieved quite effectively with the woodcut or the collage relief print. The print can be designed specifically for embossing alone or can combine embossing with the use of color in the oil base or the water base method. When color is to be used in the print the embossing should be the last operation. The paper is so sensitive to the depressions in the wood that even delicate woodcut strokes, holes, and textures appear strongly embossed.

A heavy Japanese paper takes embossing best because the fibers are pliable and there is less risk from tearing. We have found that Torinoko, Kochi, and Masa papers give excellent results. Dampen the paper slightly by dipping it into water and removing it immediately. Blot it well between dry blotters. The paper should be almost dry. It is also possible to emboss without dampening the paper but there is greater danger from tearing. Place the paper on the block. Use the register frame if other colors have been printed first. Press firmly into the recessions with a curved chrome burnisher used in etching. Take care not to tear the paper. We have found the burnisher works very well because it can be forced into small places and has smooth sides that do not mar the paper. If the point on the burnisher is ground down and dulled there will be no danger of tearing. The Japanese sometimes use the elbow for pressing the paper into the recessions on the block. This method works amazingly well.

COLLAGE RELIEF PRINT

The freedom of today's artist to use a wide range of materials is almost endless since the early collage experiments of the Dadaists, Braque, Picasso, and Schwitters. The new vitality in printmaking owes an obvious debt to this tradition of experimentation and unorthodoxy in visual expression.

The relief print has been very adaptable to new materials and experimental means. "If it can be inked, it can be printed" is the only rule. This rule leaves the relief print open to endless possibilities, including found objects like charred discarded wood, driftwood, intricate printed circuits, crushed tin cans, and container lids. It leaves open the possibility of inking and printing anything from a manhole cover to a weathered door of a barn. During some of our experi-

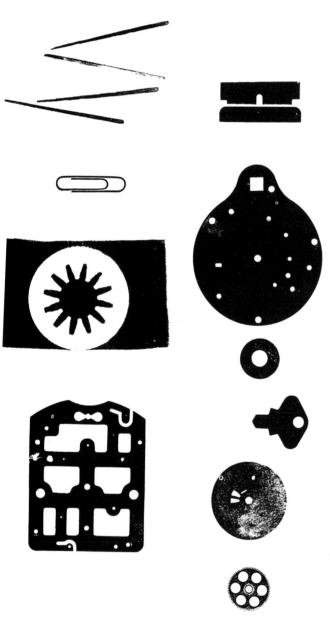

Relief rolled found objects tooth picks, paper clip, electronic copper disk, clock part. Printed on an etching press.

Relief rolled found objects: razor blade, flat machine part, washer, luggage key, electronic disk, clock gear all printed on an etching press.

Crayon rubbing of manhole cover.

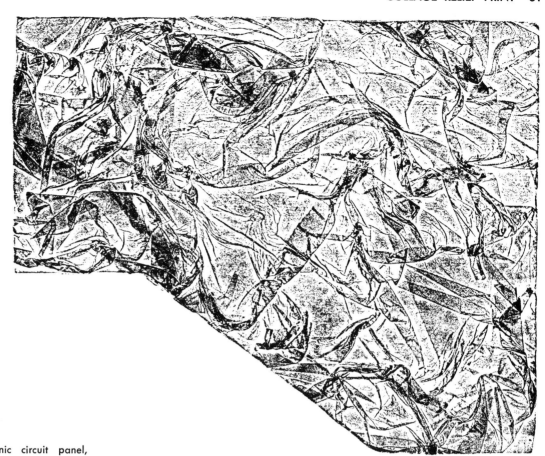

Relief rolled crumpled bond paper gessoed onto a carboard backing.

Below: Relief rolled electronic circuit panel, copper on plastic by Techniques, Inc., Englewood, New Jersey.

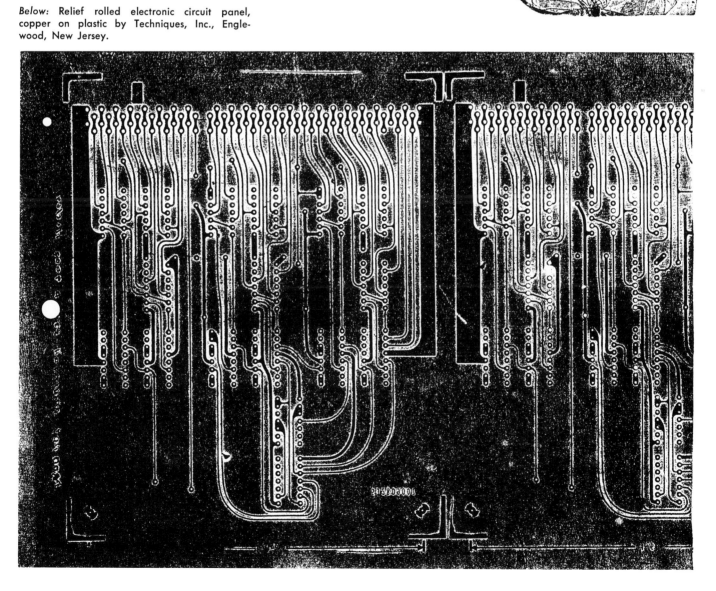

Relief rolled commercial greeting cards.

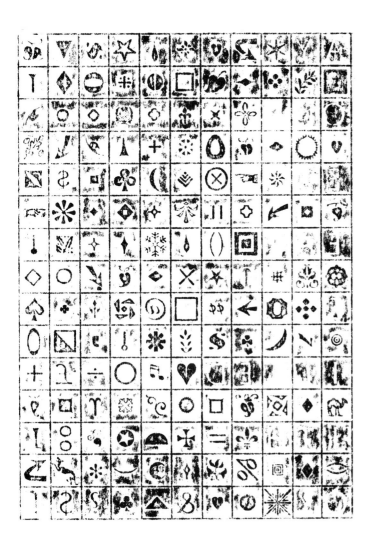

mentation with unorthodox materials, one student inked his own face with a soft roller and printed himself with quite interesting results. The wisest procedure is to gather objects and store them for future use. Seeing the assembled objects together can often give the artist ideas for images. Sometimes transformations such as hammering out metal objects in order to print them more easily is desirable. Some systemizing in the collecting can also be useful. Organic materials such as wood, rocks, slate, and plant forms can be collected, inked, and proofed to see what possibilities may be inherent in each object. Technological materials gathered together can be very suggestive; gaskets, gears, parts of clocks, screening, plastics, machinery, tin, aluminum, or copper that can be cut with a pair of shears can be intriguing in form. Soft materials such as cloth, dust, sand, tubed solder, metal particles, lace, string, oilcloth, or embroidery produce completely different images. These soft materials and organic materials such as grasses and plant forms can be soaked in acrylic liquids and hardened and printed as single units or glued down immediately with Elmer's glue or gesso. The printing of a whole group of objects with great variation in texture and form can develop a rich amount of source material that can be cut out. These images can be manipulated into compositions to explore their possibilities more easily as printed areas than as objects. After the relationships of objects are determined, their silhouettes can be traced on cardboard or Masonite in order to position them, or they can be glued to a board for more permanence during the printing of the edition. Experimentation and inventiveness are the key. Without them the objects merely become prints of themselves without any transformation. Michael Rothenstein, the English printmaker, has used found objects imaginatively in many of his prints.

Printing the Collage Print

The printing procedures for collage prints are not much different from those of the woodcut, except that the collage print, because of its porous and varied surfaces, requires more inking and softer rollers. For very rough surfaces, a soft ink and a soft roller will help to achieve the nuances of surface textures. A fairly absorbent, sensitive paper is also good to use for best results. If the paper is thin, a second sheet may be needed between the print image and the burnisher to keep it from tearing. Often, the use of the hand and fingers is sufficient to print rough surfaces, and a wooden burnisher can be used for smooth areas. If the paper to be used is quite thick, dampening it lightly and blotting it well may help to make it more supple and malleable around uneven surfaces. In all instances care must be taken to keep the paper from tearing.

Hard rubber roller. Printed on an etching press.

Relief rolled traffic sign. Printed on the back of translucent paper through an etching press.

Relief rolled traffic sign printed on the top of paper laid over the embossed metal sign.

Broken glass, inked and printed by rubbing.

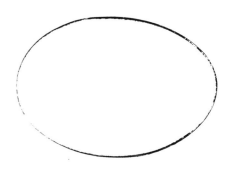

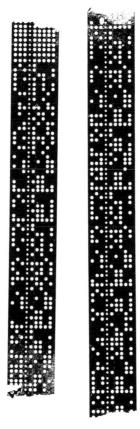

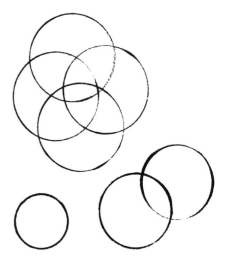

Relief rolled paper computer tapes, printed on an etching press.

Stamped prints made from wooden numbers and a cut cardboard sun shape.

Relief rolled Yugoslavian coins. Printed on an etching press.

Stamped prints made from the bottoms of glass jars of different shapes. The lower group is printed from the inked heads of flat-head wood screws.

Below: Prints made from dried glue and other adhesives; from left to right; Plastic Wood, Ceramic Glue, Liquid Aluminum, Miracle Adhesive, Liquid Solder, Duco Cement, Liquid Steel, and Thermogrip Glue.

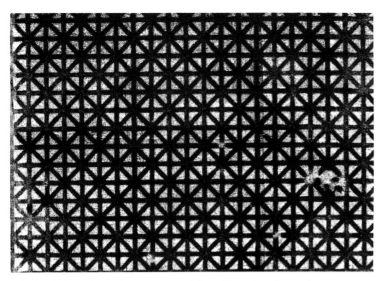

Relief rolled perforated screen printed by rolling directly on the paper laid on top of the screen.

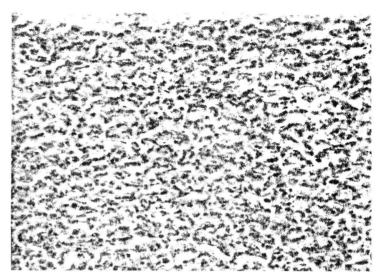

Relief rolled textured glass. Spoon printed.

Relief rolled aluminum perforated screen. Printed on an etching press.

Same perforated screen used as a stencil to protect the paper. Printed with a rag and dilute ink.

Relief rolled wooden french curves. Printed on an etching press.

Relief rolled wooden french curves printed on the top of paper laid over the objects.

Metal gasket used as a stencil. Dilute ink is applied with a rag.

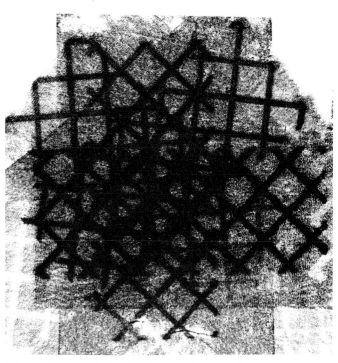

Relief rolled zinc block printed by rolling a hard rubber brayer on top of the paper laid over the block. Four printings with Japanese rice spoon.

Relief rolled directly on to paper using gasket as a stencil to protect the paper.

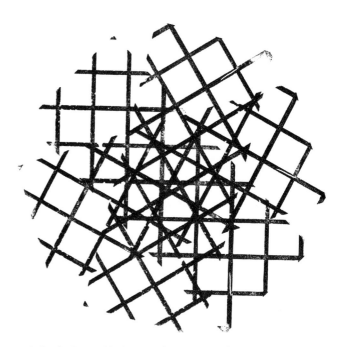

Relief rolled zinc block printed three times by spoon printing.

Relief rolled metal gasket printed on an etching press.

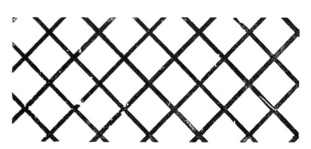

Relief rolled zinc block used as a support for photoengravings. Spoon printed.

CARDBOARD RELIEF PRINT

The flexibility of cardboard, its ease of cutting, and its availability make it an ideal material for a relief print. If two- or three-ply chip board is used, it can be handled very much like wood itself. Sharp tools are needed for cutting. We have found the best tools to be industrial single-edge razor blades, which can be discarded when they are dull. An exacto knife with blades that can be resharpened is suitable for fine detail cutting, though cardboard is not particularly suited for very fine work. The cardboard can be cut into and peeled away very much as wood is cut. Sometimes the lower surface can be inked and printed if that enhances the composition. It is best to cut areas with some angulation away from the edge of the form, just as wood is handled, so that the form does not break away in printing. Textures can be hammered or scratched into the cardboard with a variety of instruments from a dressmaker's wheel to punches and rasps.

A freer use of the cardboard relief can be achieved by cutting all the forms out completely, arranging them on a piece of three-ply cardboard or ⅛" Masonite until the relationships are satisfactory, and then gluing them down with Elmer's glue or gesso or lacquer and coating them to seal the surfaces. Papers of various thickness, in addition to cardboards of different thickness from three-ply chip board to mat board to shirt cardboards used by laundries, can be used. Masking tape also makes a quick, easy material to build up linear structures.

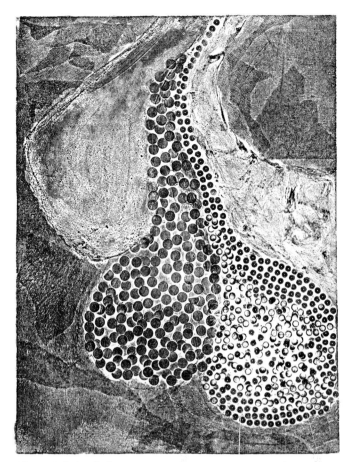

Above: Relief rolled sequins, paper tissues, paper towels, sand in wet gesso on mat board. Printed on an etching press by Kathleen Dixon, Manhattanville College.

Relief rolled cut paper and cardboard, paper toweling on cardboard. Four blocks by R. Fontaine of Pratt Institute, Brooklyn.

Left: Relief rolled towel, fabric, crumpled paper, and paper strips on pebbled mat board. C. Witko, Pratt Institute, Brooklyn.

Seal both the cardboard relief print and the collage print with plastic spray, diluted Elmer's glue, gesso, or lacquer. If this is not carefully done the whole composition will break down during inking and cleaning with solvents after printing. Sometimes the sealing of the surface can become structural if gesso is used undiluted. The brush strokes become integral parts of the form. Cutting cardboard away for some forms and painting the image with gesso to utilize other forms can become a very free way to work. The gesso should be fairly thick if it is to print as a structural image.

The cardboard and the collage prints present unique opportunities to exploit texture and surface. Varied color textures printed over each other can develop the color quality with great richness.

Edmond Casarella
"Blaze of Glory"
Color cardboard cut 13" x 15"
Courtesy of the artist

Printing the Cardboard Relief

Printing the cardboard relief print is not too different from printing the woodcut. Although the surface of the cardboard print must be well sealed, it is still a more absorbent surface than wood and will take a little more ink. The soft rollers suggested for the collage print are very good. Sometimes just hand rubbing without a burnisher is all that is necessary because of the softer color inks and the softer surface of the cardboard relief print.

Cardboard to Repair a Woodcut

The use of cardboard as a relief material can have a dual purpose. It can be used with great individuality as a means of expression on its own, and it can also be used very efficiently in combination with the woodcut to make additional plates or to make corrections. There are times when a key block of some complexity is cut out of wood and additional colors with simpler forms are cut out of cardboard. In such instances, using cardboard for the color areas would be very logical and easy. It also is very helpful to use cardboard to repair an area, by shaving down the wood and inserting cardboard. Mat board or chip board in two or three ply may be used. It is important to glue the areas down securely with Elmer's glue or gesso and to spray the surface with plastic spray or to brush on diluted Elmer's glue or gesso.

WOOD VENEER AND BALSA WOOD COLLAGE PRINT

Wood veneers in a variety of grains can be used very successfully in developing a wood relief collage that can be inked and printed as an ordinary woodcut. The veneers can be glued to any rigid surface, such as ¼″ Masonite or ¼″ plywood. We have had students glue the veneers with gesso or animal glue to ¼″ plywood and after the gluing was completed, proceed to cut and develop both the glued veneer and the plywood upon which it was glued with interesting effects. Balsa wood, used in model building, can also be used particularly well for geometric concepts. The balsa comes in a wide range of strip sizes and thicknesses and is readily available in art supply stores, especially where architecture students trade. The balsa, though very soft, can be cut and gouged after gluing.

MASONITE RELIEF PRINT

Masonite can be used with some success for the relief print. The hard-tempered Masonite works best. There is a soft-tempered kind that is not advisable because it cannot be cut well. When hard-tempered Masonite is used, ordinary woodcutting tools can be manipulated easily enough if they are kept very sharp. One side of the Masonite is very smooth and can be utilized for fairly detailed cutting. The other side has a texture that resembles a weave and can be developed as textural surface however, it can become monotonous. Some artists find Masonite more expressive with color, as

the textural and linear range of the material is certainly less than the potential of the black and white woodcut.

Power tools can be handled with success in enriching the surface and imposing textural qualities on either side. They can also be used on the smooth side to develop linear and structural imagery. Masonite has considerable potential as an intaglio plate.

GESSO OR PLASTER PRINT

A very fast way of working in the relief print is to use plaster as a basic material for the block. When the plaster is semi-dry, it is quite workable with a variety of tools, and images and textures can be developed with remarkable ease. The technique is fairly simple and requires no special skill or equipment.

Place a piece of plexiglas, lucite, ¼″ plate glass, formica, or any smooth-surfaced, flat material on a table. Make a frame of 1″ by 2″ or 1″ by 3″ lumber and lay it flat on the plexiglas, arranged to fit the size of block that you want to make. You may use masking tape to hold the frame in position.

Use a large mixing bowl or pail to mix enough plaster to cover your plate to a depth of ¾″. Add the plaster to the water in a pail large enough to permit stirring. Use ordinary builders' plaster and mix well with a stick. It should be thin enough to pour.

Pour one half of your mixture onto the plexiglas. The smooth surface will make the printing surface of your dried plaster block. When half the mixture has been poured into the frame, put the pail aside and place a piece of aluminum or copper window screening, previously cut to fit your block, on the wet plaster. It should be slightly smaller than the finished block. This mesh will act as a stiffener and internal brace for the plaster and will give it strength and resistance to breaking. When your screening is in place, pour the remaining plaster into the frame. The screening will be sandwiched between the layers of wet plaster. After 20 minutes or so, the plaster will feel hot. It may be removed from the frame at this time. While it is soft, scratch into it or work in whatever manner you choose with nails, needles, screws, and the like. Because plaster dries rather slowly, the time that you have to work on the damp block will vary with the temperature. It would be helpful to brush the smooth surface of the plaster with a coat of India ink. When you scrape or scratch the surface, each mark will be clearly visible. You can work with great speed on the block while it is damp. When plaster is dry it becomes very hard and will yield fine detail and thin lines. If you want to soften the block after it is dry, soak it in water for 5 or 10 minutes to restore some of the qualities of easily cut new plaster.

To make a plaster block, Richard Otreba of Poland constructs a frame of 1″ by 2″ furring strips arranged around a flat sheet of plexiglas or lucite.

Otreba pours plaster into the form made by the wood strips and the sheet plastic. A piece of screening or wire mesh is placed in the wet plaster to give it strength. Before the plaster has completely hardened it may be scratched or incised easily.

Opposite:
John Ross
"Duomo" 1959
Cardboard relief 29½″ x 22¼″
Collection Cincinnati Museum

Arthur Deshaies
"Cycle of a Large Sea: Unbeing myself" 1961
Plaster relief engraving 54" x 36¾"
Brooklyn Museum

If you have overcut an area or want to fill some lines, add new plaster with a palette knife, let it harden, and sand it smooth with fine sandpaper.

Before printing the plaster block, seal the surface by spraying with a few coats of clear lacquer. This seal will make the block easier to clean and will toughen the surface for the brayer and the inking. The printing should be accomplished by hand rubbing only. Any press printing will probably split the brittle plaster and crack it beyond repair.

GLUE PRINT

Certain adhesives and glues that dry to a hard consistency and do not dissolve in the solvents used to clean oil-based inks may be used as textures or linear images. They include Plastic Wood, Miracle Adhesive, Liquid Steel, Liquid Aluminum, Duco Cement, wood putty, polymer acrylic gesso, modelling paste, and many other products.

THE STAMPED PRINT

Many surfaces may be inked and printed. Bottle caps, wine corks, jar bottoms, machine parts, wooden numbers and sign-makers letters, and other found objects can be printed but are too bulky or awkward to be glued in position on a base board. Make a cardboard or oak-tag position sheet, cut holes in it where you want to print a particular shape, and use this position sheet as a guide for printing, directly on the finished print, whatever shape you choose. Simply stamp the shape onto the paper, using adequate pressure and a few blotters or newsprint sheets under the paper to act as a cushion. Repeat patterns can be attained quickly and with little trouble by using stamped shapes.

You may cut simple forms into Ruby erasers and even Art Gum erasers. These make wonderful little stamps, and repeats are easy with them. You can quickly make a forest by cutting two or three trees from erasers or small wood or cardboard pieces. These stamps may be inked with rollers, with conventional stamp pads, or by rolling out color onto a slab, pressing the shape into the color, and then stamping it onto your print.

THE MONOPRINT

Materials

Printing ink, oil colors, water colors, brushes, rags, sponge, sticks, metal tools, cardboard squares, rollers, medium-weight paper for stencils, any non-absorbent material such as glass, lucite, formica, masonite, rice paper or any fairly absorbent paper, mineral spirits, rubbing tools.

The monoprint is exactly what the word indicates. It is a one-print method. An image is made on a nonabsorbent surface, such as glass, with inks or paints and transferred onto a piece of fairly absorbent paper by placing the sheet of paper on the prepared surface and rubbing the back with the hand or a rubbing tool. The monoprint is a unique image and cannot be duplicated, nor can an edition be made as in other printmaking medias. Because the image cannot be reprinted, it is not considered a print image and is most often barred from print exhibitions. However, as it does produce very unusual results, somewhere between the print and painting, it deserves a place in this section. It is also a good way to quickly realize the idea of the printed image, the reversal of the image and the rubbing of a relief block.

Anyone who has cleaned off a painter's palette of many colors knows that in the process of cleaning off the palette with a palette knife very beautiful color qualities take shape.

A three-dimensional assemblage of cast plaster impressions from Antonio Frasconi's inked wood cuts.

Below: A number of small wood blocks are cast in plaster, making embossed impressions, forming a single unit by Antonio Frasconi.

Adhesives, cement, and glues that harden when dry. They may be inked and printed. Included are materials available in most hardware stores, such as plastic wood, Duco cement, liquid steel, and aluminum. The device at the right is a heat-operated glue gun. See page 64 for print of these adhesives.

If at that moment a piece of rice paper were dropped onto the palette and rubbed with the hand or a rubbing tool, a close duplication of the palette image would be transferred to the paper. The monoprint can be as free as that, color strewn on a nonabsorbent surface and drawn into with stick or sharp tool or manipulated with a rag, or mineral spirits used to help move the colors around and create blending effects.

The monoprint can also be approached in a very painterly manner with the image painted in numerous colors directly on the smooth surface with a variety of brushes and then printed. If necessary a sketch can be prepared on paper and used as a guide by slipping it under a piece of glass and the color applied with brushes or rags or rollers on the glass surface. This method can allow a number of prints to be printed with some controlled uniformity. Printing paper can also be held in position by being taped to the smooth surface of glass or other material while color is applied and printed in two or three sequential printings that allow overprinting effects. The taping will insure accurate registry.

Rollers can be used to roll a single color or many colors onto the printing surface, and an image can be drawn into the inked area with sticks, metal tools, or cardboard cards.

Cut or torn paper shapes can also be placed on the rolled ink surface to combine the monoprint with a stencil print.

Another very interesting use of the monoprint is to combine it with a partially worked plate. An etching plate, lithograph plate or stone, or woodcut can be developed to a certain point, after which painted or drawn material can be added to the plate or stone. It can then be run through the etching or lithograph press or, if wood is used, rubbed by hand to produce the softness of a painted image with the qualities of the print.

Michael Mazur paints directly on an etching plate with ink and turps and combines cut plates and embossing to produce unique images.

Michael Mazur
"Artist-Model and Studio View" 1968
Cut plate monoprint 15⅞" x 31¾"
Terry Dintenfass Gallery, New York

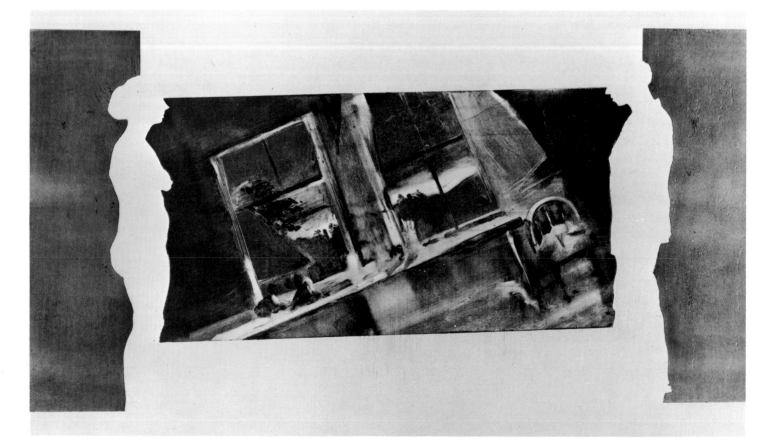

PRINTMAKING FOR CHILDREN

INTRODUCTION

We have included this section on printmaking for children for a number of reasons. We know from our own experience how our sons enjoyed many hours working alongside us in our printmaking studio from the time they could hold tools. We know the value and joy of their early endeavors with printmaking. Now that they are older, their knowledge of printmaking has produced two helpful printers for edition printing. Numerous friends who teach elementary and junior high school art classes often come to us to ask how they can adapt some of our techniques and materials for use in their children's classes. Essentially, the methods we list on the following pages are relief print methods and should relate to children from the ages of six to thirteen. High school children from the ages of fourteen to eighteen should be able to utilize the adult approach in the main body of this book as long as they show a strong interest and are supervised. Many high school art departments are extremely well equipped and often have both etching and lithograph presses and offer highly sophisticated programs. In our New School and Art Center classes, which are run on a workshop basis, whether for credit or not, we have occasionally had gifted young people of fifteen or sixteen who showed remarkable feeling for printmaking and were a welcome and inspiring addition to an adult class.

The merits of introducing printmaking to the very young are many. The experience of expressing themselves in another medium and developing their tactile sense is especially important. The combined quality of the constructed or cut-away surface gives them a sense of the bas relief and is a fine way to lead them on to explore three-dimensional construction and sculpture. The magic of the print process through the inking of a surface and the production of an image that is not drawn or painted is an exciting experience for them.

An excellent way to introduce the concept of the print to very young children from six to eight is to have them make monoprints. Although the monoprint is not a true print medium because it cannot be duplicated, it does show quickly how an impression can be made from an inked surface. We have found that another excellent way to introduce the print to this age group is to have them experience a new place, by taking a walk or an excursion to gather objects that can be inked and printed. Our son Tim's early experiences at the seashore each summer and his insatiable appetite for scavenging shells, pebbles, and the flotsam and jetsam of the sea led him to assembling the objects, gluing them on a cardboard, printing them, and then making a color woodcut of his own interpretation of the shells and the sea.

The tools given to young children must of course be carefully selected. Sharp tools must be eliminated unless groups are very small and carefully supervised. Simple, easily obtainable materials are best. Water-based inks are always available and easy to clean up. Oil-based inks are excellent because they do not dry too quickly, allowing more time to ink surfaces; but they are harder to clean up and present added problems when clothing gets into the ink. For cutting linoleum and wood, it would be best to eliminate knives except for older children who are closely supervised. Gouges for cutting are very satisfactory as long as the child is taught to keep the non-cutting hand behind the cutting one. The bench hook for holding the block discussed in the section on the relief print is a useful aid in cutting and helps to avoid cutting accidents. In each of the following methods we do list all the simple tools required. However, as all the methods are relief methods it would be helpful to read the material in the section on the relief print.

MONOPRINT (All Ages)

Materials

A smooth, nonabsorbent surface such as glass, lucite, Masonite, enamel pan, linoleum, or vinyl can be used for drawing the monoprint.

Water-based or oil-based ink or paint
Flat sticks or brushes for painting
Palette knife, rollers, rags
Newsprint paper, kitchen wooden spoon for rubbing print
Water or mineral spirits for clean up

The monoprint can be quick and spontaneous, depending on textural qualities, or it can be thoughtful and painterly, and it usually produces interesting results. The monoprint is exactly what the word indicates. It is one print, taken from a design developed or drawn by a variety of means on a hard, nonabsorbent surface with either water-based or oil-based inks or paint. A sheet of paper is then placed over the image, and the paper is rubbed by the hand, a soft rag, or a spoon, and an impression or *monoprint* is printed on the paper.

Numerous colors can be applied, by brush or by roller. A palette knife can blend colors, and mineral spirits can be poured or dabbed onto the surface to achieve blending or running effects in the colors. If a brush is used, a free, painterly drawing with numerous colors can be made. Fingers, rags, sticks, and rollers can also be employed to draw into the colors.

Still another method, similar to stencil printing, is to lay thin cut-out paper shapes on an inked surface of one or many colors and to take an impression of the partially masked surface. The paper shapes will print as open white forms with color around them.

Monoprint
Image painted on glass with stiff brush and printing ink thinned with mineral spirits. Grass texture made with stick drawn through ink.
James, age, 11

OBJECT PRINT (All Ages)

Materials

Shells, flat pebbles, leaves, feathers, coins, embossings, and so on.

Wood in a variety of shapes and textures, cut to shapes or from old packing cases, driftwood, and the like.

Stamped metal grating, flattened tin cans, bottle tops, raised letters, old plastic blocks, and other materials.

Water-based or oil-based inks, soft rollers, a spoon for rubbing.

Newsprint paper or rice paper (Rice paper has a soft absorbent quality that makes it receptive for printing hard objects. Troya is a soft domestic paper that works well. Tableau, a paper made in Boston for filters and sold in rolls, is relatively inexpensive and very good. Check supply sources at back of book.).

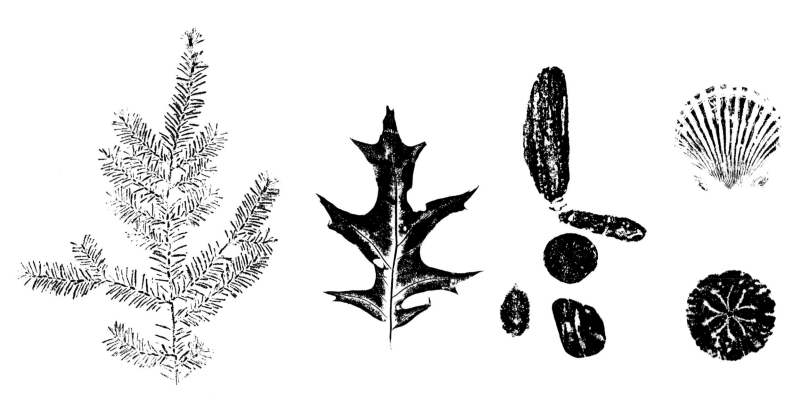

Object Print
Pebbles, Shells, Oak Leaf, Hemlock branch.
Mary and Ruth, ages eight and nine

A smooth inking palette can be any nonabsorbent, easily cleaned material: glass, lucite, masonite, enamel pan, and so on.

Rags, water, or mineral spirits for cleaning up, depending on whether water or oil-based inks are used; palette knives to clean palettes.

If an object has a flat enough surface, to receive the roller, it can be inked and printed. Avoid sharp or especially rough surfaces because they will be hard to ink and will tear the paper.

Ink objects with a variety of colors, place a sheet of paper over the inked objects, and rub it with fingers or spoon. Print either on single sheets or in a variety of arrangements on a large piece of paper. Impressions made on small papers can be cut out and pasted down on a large sheet of paper for a small mural.

OFFSET ROLLER PRINT

Materials

2 soft rollers, 2″ or 3″ in diameter
Some interesting textured object
Water-based or oil-based ink
Newsprint paper

Inking palette, palette knives, rags, water or mineral spirits

A variation of object printing is to ink an intricate object with a roller until a good quantity of ink is built up on the surface. Take a second clean roller and run it across the ob-

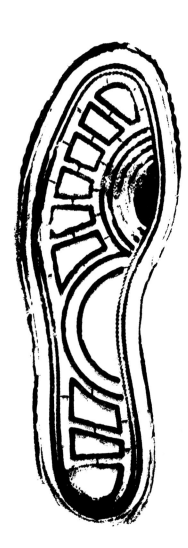

Offset Roller Print
Bottom of a child's sneaker rolled with a heavy build up of ink. Clean, soft roller rolled over inked sneaker, picking up pattern on clean roller, and rolled on to paper.
Robert, age nine

ject. The clean roller will pick up an impression from the inked intricate surface. Now roll out the impression on the clean roller onto a piece of newsprint paper. The image will offset the object's image onto the paper.

STENCIL PRINT
(All Ages, Simplified for Young Children)

Materials

Thin, stiff bristol board, scissors
One or two soft rollers
Water-based or oil-based inks, inking palette
Newsprint paper
Rags, solvent or water for clean-up

Following the principle of stencil printing, cut the image to be printed out of the stencil paper. Tape the stencil on to a table. Slip a sheet of newsprint paper under the stencil. Roll an inked roller across the open surface to produce the print. If stencil areas are isolated, more than one color, each with its roller, can be used. Older children might make a two-color stencil with two stencils by taping the stencils, carefully cut to register, onto a cardboard with four cardboard stops glued to the cardboard to serve as paper guides.

Stencil Print
Cars drawn on stiff paper cut out with small scissors.
Ellen, Age 6

CARDBOARD AND PAPER PRINT (All Ages)

Materials

Shirt cardboard (thin cardboard used in laundries to package shirts), corrugated board, two-ply chip board, stiff paper

Elmer's glue, brushes, inking palette, rollers, oil-based or water-based ink

Cardboard and Paper Print
Heads cut out of shirt cardboard and paper,
glued with Elmer's glue, and left
as a silouhetted relief.
Louisa, age 13

Rags, mineral spirits or water, texture tools such as a dressmaker's wheel, a rasp, and so on.

For older children, 9-13, X-acto knives with a variety of blades

Cut images out of thin cardboard and paper with scissors. Glue shapes down on two-ply chip board or corrugated board with Elmer's glue. Coat the surface of the plate with a dilute mixture of Elmer's glue: $\frac{1}{3}$ water and $\frac{2}{3}$ Elmer's glue. Be sure that all the cardboard forms are well glued and the surface is dry before printing. It is necessary to coat the cardboard surface with the dilute mixture to seal the surface; if this is not done the cardboard will disintegrate and peel up during inking.

In a well-supervised small group, older children can be allowed to cut into two- or three-ply chip board or corrugated board with an X-acto knife. A drawing or guide lines can be made right on the board with a soft pencil. The cardboard can then be cut and peeled away from around the form, leaving the image in high relief. Textures can be hammered and rubbed into the surface with anything that can make a mark, such as a dressmaker's marking wheel, a pizza cutter, a rasp, or bottle caps hammered into the cardboard to make impressions that will print. Coat the whole surface of the plate with dilute Elmer's glue to seal the surface. Ink it and print it.

COLLAGE PRINT (All Ages)

Materials

Cloth of various textures, lace, actual pieces of clothing such as a boy's shirt, part of a pair of dungarees, paper in various textures, flat sticks such as popsicle sticks, scraps of thin, flat wood, string, sand, sawdust, cat litter, metal mesh grating, wire mesh, crushed tinfoil, oil cloth, sandpaper, beans, noodles, scotch tape, masking tape, and other materials.

Stiff cardboard or thin Masonite on which to glue the materials

Scissors, Elmer's glue, acrylic gesso, polymer medium, inking palette, newsprint paper, Troya, filter paper, soft rollers in a variety of sizes, a rubbing spoon.

Water or mineral spirits for clean-up, oil-based or water-based inks

The collage print is a most versatile print medium. It affords a great textural experience for children because the materials can be selected by them and used with a thought to building a design through textures. The only limitation is whether or not an object or materials can be glued down and inked. If it can be inked, it can be printed.

The plate can be developed by making a sketch in pencil on the cardboard or Masonite backing board. Glue down the materials in relation to the sketch with Elmer's glue or acrylic gesso. Be sure the materials are adhered well to the backing. A thin coat of dilute Elmer's glue should be applied to the entire surface. The plate can also be made by just a free assemblage of interesting textures and forms, without any sketch. Be sure the plate is thoroughly dry before inking. An overnight wait may be advisable. Small soft rollers should be used for inking and the ink applied generously because

Collage Print
Paper clip, rubber bands, cloth,
string, subway token, nuts,
glued to cardboard with Elmer's glue.
Michael, age 12

the textured nature of most of the material requires more ink than a hard surface.

Interesting prints can be made by gluing down pieces of clothing such as a man's shirt or part of a pair of dungarees on a stiff backing with Elmer's glue or gesso. A whole garment can even be immersed in polymer medium, glued to a backing, allowed to dry, and printed.

Masking tape and cellophane tape can be used to build interesting linear plates. Beans, noodles, or string can be used for background textures and to build a whole image. Sand and sandpaper and sawdust can also be used for textures. The textured images produce some surprises when printed. Smooth surfaces such as oilcloth and smooth paper print very black, while textured surfaces such as sand and sandpaper and corduroy fabric print with light textures.

Different colors on small rollers can be used to ink the same plate to produce a colorful print. During printing, rub the back of the paper well with your hand, a rubbing spoon, or a rag rolled into a ball, depending on the material to be printed. Use soft rice paper such as Troya, Mulberry, or filter paper because it is more pliable than newsprint. However, if only newsprint is available, it will produce adequate results.

Woodcut
Woodcut cut with simple
Japanese tools in soft pine.
Martha, age, 11

WOODCUT, LINOLEUM, HEAVY VINYL, AND BALSA-WOOD PRINTS (All Ages)

Materials

Linoleum, heavy vinyl, knotty pine, balsa wood. Buy heavy-duty linoleum, and vinyl unbacked in a floor covering store. It is less expensive than the mounted kind found in art supply stores. The pine can be obtained in a lumber yard in 8″ shelf widths cut to size. Scraps are often obtainable free of charge. Balsa wood used in model building can be found in art supply stores.

Inexpensive Japanese woodcut tools sold in small wooden boxes in many art supply stores or Japanese novelty shops are very good. They usually include a gouge or two, a knife, a chisel, and a sharpening stone. Do not buy the plastic bagged kind sold in dime stores. They break easily.

Though we do not suggest the Speedball tools for adults, the sets made with removable nibs are adequate for children.

Wire brushes, stamping objects, rasps, oil-based or water-based ink, soft rollers, inking palette, bench hook, newsprint paper, water or mineral spirits for clean-up, rags.

Simple designs and drawings can be cut in linoleum or wood if the child is shown how to carefully handle the tools, always keeping the supporting hand behind the cutting hand. Use a bench hook to hold the block. Check the woodcut equipment section for instructions on how to make one. It is a simple device and easy to use.

When using wood, select soft, easily cut pieces. Some lumber yards are very sympathetic to the idea that their scraps can be used for woodcuts and often give large quantities to schools. Blacken the wood surface with some dilute India ink or printing ink so that the cutting can be easily seen. White chalk can be used to indicate a design. The children can begin by selecting a piece of wood that has an interesting grain or knots. The grain can be made more visible by rubbing a steel brush into it to wear down the soft areas and allow the grainy ridges to stand out. Sometimes the wood itself will suggest a landscape or features of a figure will seem apparent in the distribution of knots.

Use simple gouges at first for cutting. Try stamping and pounding textures into the wood and printing them. This is very easy with balsa wood and pine shelving.

The linoleum and vinyl are easier to cut than the wood and can be cut with simple gouges for quick results.

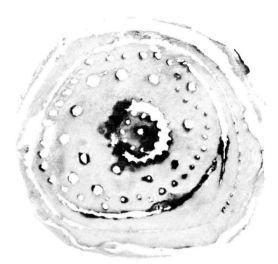

3M VINYL
LUCITE and ACETATE PRINTS

A new material produced by the Minnesota Mining and Manufacturing Company is quite a fine print material. It is thin enough to be cut with scissors and can be cut with gouges. It is called 3M vinyl.

Heavy acetate and vinyl can be cut with scissors and scratched into with old dental tools or any sharp instrument. Very good prints can be made from the round vinyl tops used on coffee cans. Cut away the ridge and you will have a good material to scratch, gouge or cut with scissors. The interesting quality of the 3M material and the vinyl and acetate is that pieces of these materials can be cut in many parts, inked separately, then reassembled and printed at one time.

PLASTICINE PRINT (Young Children)

Materials

Plasticine, oil-based ink, soft roller, inking palette, rubbing spoon, newsprint paper, solvents, interesting objects to press into plasticine such as bottle caps, coins, textured objects, and so on.

Simple prints can be made by flattening some plasticine with a roller or pressing it with a piece of wood, to about ⅛" thickness. Press any interesting objects into it to make an impression, or draw into it with a sharp tool such as the back of a brush. Roll ink over the surface, using oil-based ink because the oily plasticine may repel the water-based ink. Place the paper over the inked surface of the plasticine and rub the back of the paper with your hand or softly with a spoon so that the plasticine images are not crushed.

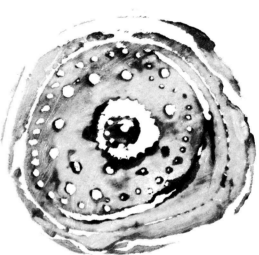

Plasticine Print
Shapes flattened out, punctured and scored with a stick.
Charles, age, 6

GLUE PRINT (All Ages)

Materials

Elmer's glue, acrylic gesso, cardboard, oil-based and water-based ink, soft and bristle brushes, cardboard cut in 2" squares for drawing linear images, inking palette, soft rollers, solvent or water for clean-up, newsprint paper, rags

Very interesting prints can be made with glue or acrylic gesso. Elmer's glue can be squeezed right out of its plastic container and used as a drawing tool or be dripped or painted on a cardboard backing, allowed to dry, then given a thin coating of dilute Elmer's glue, inked, and printed.

Glue Print
Elmer's Glue squeeze bottle
used to draw and drip image.
Ellen, age, 6

More controlled images can be made by using soft and stiff brushes to paint on cardboard backing, building it up by drying and repainting so that some higher surfaces can develop. Acrylic gesso, when not too liquid, can produce some fairly good relief areas. The cardboard squares can be used to apply gesso in linear forms or, if folded, can be used to apply texture areas.

Allow the design to dry thoroughly, then coat it with a diluted Elmer's glue to seal the surface of any open cardboard areas. Ink the plate with soft rollers, place newsprint or rice paper over the surface, and rub with your hand or a spoon.

STAMP PRINT (All Ages)

Stamp Print
Leaves, and stars cut out
of soft red erasers
and cardboard.
Thomas, age, 12

Materials

Ruby erasers (any firm rubber erasers usually manufactured in a variety of colors for pencil erasing)

Two- and 3-ply cardboard, large firm potatoes, X-acto knives, paring knife, oil-based and water-based inks, inking palette, soft rollers, solvents, rags, newsprint paper.

Inventive little stamps can be made by cutting into the firm colored erasers used for pencil erasing. X-acto knives can be used to cut little designs in the flat surface of the erasers. Heavy layered cardboard can also be cut and peeled away to produce a simple high relief design. Attach a little handle made of masking tape to the stamp and ink the image either by tapping it in some ink rolled out on an inking palette or surface-roll the ink onto the relief surface of the stamp. Stamp the design in multiple colors, repeats, and overlaps on newsprint paper with some newspaper padding under it to insure a sharp image.

Another old, quick, simple method for very young children is to make stamps from potatoes. A simple design can be cut into halved firm potatoes with a not-too-sharp paring knife. Water-based ink can be rolled onto the relief surface of the design, or the potato stamp can be tapped into ink rolled out on an inking palette. The printing can proceed as just discussed.

CARE
OF PRINTS

MOUNTING PRINTS

Because prints are generally printed on paper, a relatively fragile substance, special care is necessary to preserve them. If a print is going to be sent to an exhibition or even displayed in your studio, a proper mat is an important part of its presentation.

The preparation of the mat is twofold because a mat actually consists of the backing board and the mat. The mat can be hinged to the backing with gummed paper tape for temporary mounting and with gummed linen tape for permanent mounting. A temporary mounting might be used if you are sending out a number of prints to many exhibitions and do not wish to incur great expense. You can use either smooth white matboard or white pebble matboard.

Most exhibitions require clean white mats for uniformity of color and good display technique. Students are sometimes carried away by the wide choice in colored matboard. Try to restrain yourself from being lured by this variety because color generally does not enhance the work.

Matting Material

The backing can be single-weight chip board for small prints and double-weight chip or corrugated board for large sizes. These backing boards are made of wood pulp and chemicals and are not recommended for permanent mounts. Over a period of time the pulp board and backing will discolor the print paper. If a print is to remain in a mounting for a long period of time or is going to be framed, 100% rag mat board and backing is necessary. Museums and reputable galleries use only rag boards for their print collections.

So many oversize prints are now being made that many exhibitions accept them without mats. The exhibiting organizations sometimes require oversize prints to be rolled and provide backing if they are accepted by the jury. Another method sometimes permissible is to back the print with double-weight white mat board cut flush to the size of the print and to wrap a medium-gauge sheet of acetate or clear vinyl around it and tape it from behind. If the double-weight mat board is not heavy enough, corrugated board or some of the new styrofoam boards are excellent because they are rigid and weigh very little; however, they are more expensive.

Measuring the Mat

The size of the mat should not be excessive. Three- to five-inch margins are fairly good as a general rule, with the 3″ size for small prints and up to 5″ for large prints. We usually make the top and side margins the same width and the bottom an inch larger. The cut-out area of the mat should be about ¼″ larger than the print size on top and sides and about ½″ larger on the bottom to allow the number, title, and signature to be easily seen.

Start by setting up a clean large measuring and cutting table. The ideal studio space should have a table just for cutting mats and wrapping packages, but that is a luxury of space few artists seem to be able to keep free. Use a large piece of chip board to top the table and to serve as a cutting board. Sharp mat knives and razor blades will soon dull if a hard, rough surface is used for cutting mats. Use a medium pencil with a good long point and do not press hard while marking, or marks may show even after erasing. Use a steel straightedge with a piece of masking tape attached to the underside to keep the straightedge from slipping. Trim both boards to size. Measure and mark off the opening to be cut.

Cutting the Mat

There are many methods for cutting a good, clean, professional mat. The important thing is to find the method that best suits you. Many students come close to hysteria at the thought of cutting a mat. Once the procedure is thought out and simplified, most people should be able to cut a reasonably good mat.

A number of varieties of good mat knives with changeable blades are sold in art supply stores. They are comfortable to hold, but we find the thickness of the blade and the constant need for sharpening a handicap. We prefer single-edge industrial razor blades, 100 to the box, fitted into a sturdy razor-blade holder obtainable in a hardware store. The razor blade is so thin and sharp and cheap that there is no excuse for a dull tool.

We often use two or three blades for one mat. Use the steel ruler as a cutting guide. Some people prefer a steel T-square. Hold down firmly on the ruler or T-square with one hand and cut straight through the board with one stroke to insure an even cut. However, if you don't have the strength for this, two or three careful cuts without moving out of the line will work. Be careful at corners and don't overcut. Some people prefer to mark and cut the mats from the back to avoid erasing and to have better control of corners. It is customary to cut the board at a slight bevel from the edge of the mat and with a little practice this should be possible. Some artists use the slanted side of the steel T-square as a guide, others use mat-cutting devices available in art supply stores.

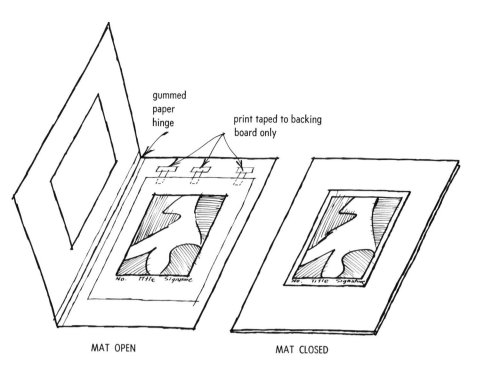

gummed paper hinge

print taped to backing board only

No. Title Signature

No. Title Signature

MAT OPEN   MAT CLOSED

Hinging Mat and Print to Backboard

After the mat is cut, hinge it to the backboard, using gummed linen tape for a permanent mat or gummed paper tape for an impermanent one. Always hinge the longest sides of the mat and backing.

The print is always attached with a hinging device to the backboard, never to the mat. First, position the print carefully with the mat in a closed position, taking care to have even spacing between the print and the edge of the mat. The print should have adequate clean margins so that there will be a sufficient margin area to allow for taping. After the print is positioned, open the mat and attach two strips of gummed linen tape about 2″ in length to the top back of the print, protruding 1″ beyond the print. Place two more strips of gummed linen tape about 3″ in length across the two protruding strips, fastening them securely to the backing. The print now hangs freely from the top only, allowing for the shrinkage and expansion caused by changing dry and humid weather. Strips for hinging may be made from the same paper used for the print. Cut strips from paper scraps and use library paste to adhere the strips to the backing. If a print is large and on heavy paper, three or four hinges might be required, with a spot of Elmer's glue to insure sticking.

Floating the Print

Another method of mounting used widely today, especially for oversized prints, is to float a print on a linen backing for framing. Some artists print their images flush to the edges of their papers, particularly in lithograph and silk-screen prints. The effect can be quite handsome when the deckle of the paper is utilized. Prepared linen boards of actual linen cloth, in a variety of textures and some tones are sold in many art supply stores. Trim the board to the correct size, and place small amounts of Elmer's glue in the two upper back corners and glue it to the backing. The bottom will hang free. The print can then be acetated for shipping to exhibitions or framed for permanence, although the print surface may be damaged by condensation on the inside of the glass.

Acetate or Vinyl Protective Covering

When you send work out to some of the smaller, less well-equipped galleries, it is well to back the prints with a sturdy backing board and to acetate them to protect them from excessive handling in print bins. A good cover is .003 gauge acetate or a clear vinyl wrapped around the print and taped to the backing. The corners can be folded with excess bulk cut away. Acetate can also be trimmed a fraction smaller than the backing and a white tape used to neatly seal the edges.

FRAMING THE PRINT

Framing a print properly is a huge specialized area. There is nothing quite as handsome as professional, first-rate framing. There are many excellent framers, particularly in large cities, and there are framing accommodations in print galleries where the people know prints and can mount and frame them properly. Avoid framers who know nothing of the proper handling of prints because they can do damage. We have seen prints trimmed unmercifully by inept framers to fit a standard mat, and we have also seen one sad job of a print that was dry-mounted to a backing, making the print impossible to remove. Find a reputable framer who specializes in prints, who has a wide selection of framing to choose from, and who will make a dustproof, tightly assembled frame.

One area of print framing that is new and must be dealt with on an individual basis is the framing of dimensional prints. If the structure is paper that has been built up through molding, cutting, or constructing, special frame boxes, usually plexiglas and sometimes glass, must be devised either by the artist himself or with a sympathetic framer. If plexiglas, metal, acetate, mylar, or any other hard nonabsorbent surface is used for the base of the actual print, it can be shown without glazing but will need some kind of mount for hanging or displaying. Vacuum-form printing makes possible a finished product of plastic material that may still be fragile because of the dimensional depth of the projecting image and, if not adequately protected, can crack or crush and be totally ruined.

Jiří Hadlac (Czechoslovakia)
"Paper with #2"
Color Woodcut
Courtesy of the artist
Photograph Josef Tichy

Glazing

A standard rule for glazing is that work done on paper must be framed under glass to prevent dirt and humidity saturation by the absorbent paper. Any glass unfortunately dulls the image somewhat but is necessary to preserve the work. Avoid glare-proof glass because it distorts the tonal quality of the print. Plexiglas is a good substitute and produces less glare than glass, but unfortunately it is expensive and must be very carefully handled because it scratches easily. Colors fade less under plexiglas than they do under glass.

Metal Section Frames

We have found an easy and less expensive substitute for commercial framing in the metal section frames available in many art supply stores and some bookstores. There are two or three varieties based on similar principles and quite simple to assemble. They are often manufactured in natural aluminum and anodized aluminum that looks golden. The glass must be purchased from a glazier and slipped into the frame.

Clare Romano
"New Jersey Turnpike"
Color Woodcut

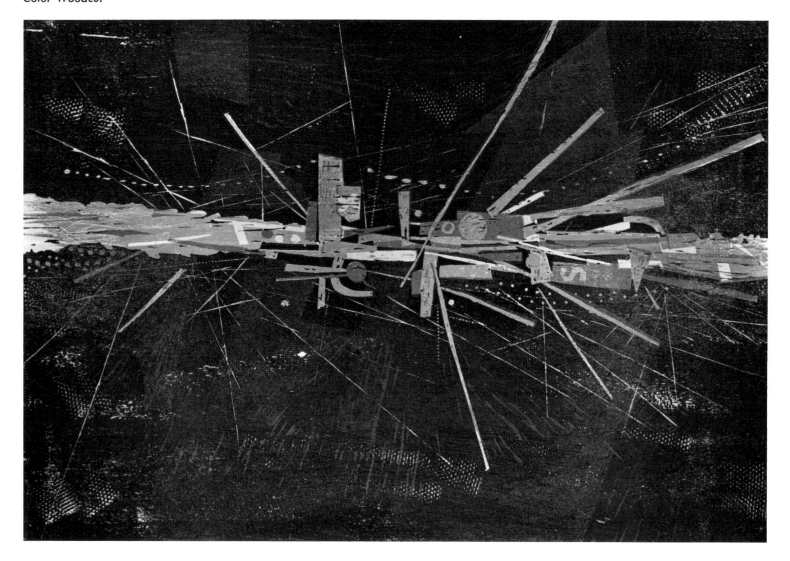

COLLECTING PRINTS

The burgeoning interest in the fine print has caused many artists to explore printmaking techniques. It has spurred galleries to exhibit and commission new prints for a new generation of print collectors. It has prompted museums to mount survey and retrospective exhibitions of contemporary and historic prints. And, to exploit this renaissance, print dealers, agents and wholesalers have sprung up like mushrooms all over the country. The print has many lovers, and new processes and techniques follow each other with increasing rapidity. It is a complex scene which greets the collector who has become intrigued by the print.

What Is An Original Print?

Definitions which once seemed to be complete, final, and absolute only a decade ago now seem ambiguous and unclear. An original print was described in a brochure issued by the Print Council in 1961 as a work of graphic art, the general requirements of which are:

1. The artist alone has made the image in or upon the plate, stone, wood block, or other material, for the purpose of creating a work of graphic art.

2. The impression is made directly from the original material by the artist or pursuant to his directions.

3. The finished print is approved by the artist.

This is still a helpful definition but it does not cover many of the situations which are arising now. The modern methods of printing, particularly in offset lithography and screen printing, have offered artists ways to create images and textures that have not been attainable in prior years.

Photographic methods that were considered reproductive are now being used by artists, with the help of skilled technicians from the commercial printing plants that abound in our mass-communicators society. Museums are accepting as original prints those impressions which would have been rejected ten or twenty years ago. The press-printed lithograph or silkscreen can be turned out in editions of thousands, and some galleries are offering color lithos in signed editions of from 3000 to 10,000 impressions. *Art in America* has printed 60,000 impressions of photographically prepared plates which are claimed to be original prints. The addition of the artist's signature is said to make the impression 100 times more valuable!

It is difficult to tell a photo-lithographic reproduction from an original lithograph, especially when the reproduction is printed on fine rag paper and has a pencilled number and a forged signature in the corner. Even well-known artists succumb to the temptation of ready cash and let craftsmen interpret watercolors, drawings and other art work into the print media. Sometimes these prints are carefully supervised by the artist but often they are not. When another artist or craftsman redraws the image on to a stone or plate the resulting print often changes in character and may distort the original drawing or design. An ethical practice would dictate that the artist-designer and the craftsman both be identified as having created the print. Some artists have been known to sign blank paper in advance of the printing of the edition. Eventually these practices will cause the discriminating collector to re-examine the prints offered for sale, with an eye to quality of impression, the strength of the image, and the size of the edition. All of these factors, plus the reputation of the artist, enter into the pricing of the print.

The print market, which in the 60's seemed to be insatiable, was affected by the general economic recession of 1970–71 and sales dropped considerably. Many galleries retrenched, some went out of business and prices of some contemporary artists either leveled off or went down. The market for old master prints held up quite well, however, and these prints are still demanding very high prices, with masterpiece prints by Rembrandt and Goya exceeding prices in six figures. The print market will undoubtedly be responsive to new changes in business and economic conditions.

Should The Collector Specialize?

The cost of amassing a good general collection of prints, with first-rate examples of great masters, is so high that only the rich can attempt it. Most people will be attracted to a certain period, or to a style, or even to an individual artist whose work they admire. A collector can restrict his interest to a single country, to a certain type of image which has special meaning to him, or in any manner which satisfies his desire to collect. Some people acquire prints as an investment against the seemingly perpetual inflation which erodes the value of currency. Certainly it is more rewarding from an esthetic point of view to study the etchings and engravings of the masters than those rather formal portraits of the presidents on paper money. The art work seems to have better durability than the cash!

In order to understand the area in which you collect it is vital to acquire some knowledge in the field. This means that the collector should first collect a few books or catalogs which describe the prints which interest him. There are catalogue raisonne's which list the entire production of an artist over his life-span. These are helpful to a serious collector who needs to know details of states and editions. Many print dealers issue catalogs which describe the prints being offered

John Ross
"Provincetown Beach"
Color Woodcut

for sale. When prices are listed these catalogs form a record of print values over the years which can be fascinating (or frustrating) to collectors. The Print Collector's Newsletter 205 East 78th Street, New York, New York 10021, is published as a bimonthly brochure in looseleaf format which gives latest prices and information on new editions of original prints. It also lists upcoming auction sales of prints as a service to its subscribers.

The way to learn about prints is to study them, find an area that interests you and then pursue that area, looking at as many prints as you can. You will then know what books and catalogs will help you in your search. If a workshop class in printmaking is available it will be helpful for the collector to enroll in order to better understand the diverse techniques which are used by artists. Many colleges and art schools offer evening courses in printmaking on a non-matriculated basis, some taught by respected and productive artists.

Where To Find Prints

Dealers have appeared all over the country. Some have elaborate gallery facilities, others operate from a closet in the hall. Some know a great deal, others know very little. A reputable, established dealer is the best source for continued acquisition of prints, of course, but sometimes a good print will appear in a gift shop, or in a decorator's boutique, or in a furniture store. When this happens, you must rely on your own knowledge and judgment as to current values. Despite recent history, print values cannot constantly go up. Therefore you should be as informed as possible in order to protect yourself from ambitious dealers or overpriced editions. Many larger companies send traveling salesmen on the road with thousands of prints, covered with acetate or vinyl, to mount one-day sales in such places as college or university galleries, libraries, or schools. Many of these exhibits contain excellent prints, but they usually include some restrikes (impressions from a plate pulled without the approval of the artist, usually after his death). There is nothing wrong with restrikes so long as they are labeled as such and it is clearly understood what they are. The general public could not afford a Durer, Goya, Rembrandt, Callot or Kollwitz if the plates were not reprinted many times. Variations in price between early and late printings of the same plate can be enormous because the plates wear rapidly, especially delicate areas such as aquatint or drypoint. Early printings have the richest blacks and the strongest tonality.

Clare Romano
"Dark Sea, Dark Sky"
Woodcut
Photograph Peter Juley

Some prints being offered for sale are cut from old magazines, such as "Verve," which were printed in very large editions (often in the thousands). These prints may be technically "originals" but should be priced accordingly.

It may be possible to buy work directly from a living artist, when you are in his neighborhood. Some artists will be distracted by this, however, and their work may be obtained only from their dealers. The most direct contact is usually the best, with the least amount of "handling" and "wholesaling" producing the best guarantee of authenticity and often the lowest prices.

A few print societies publish prints of contemporary artists, usually at favorable prices. These prints are normally restricted to members but often membership in these groups is a simple matter of joining and paying an annual fee. The Society of American Graphic Artists (S.A.G.A.) at 1083 Fifth Avenue, New York, New York 10028, offers prints by its distinguished artist members to its associate members at very low prices. The International Graphic Arts Society (I.G.A.S.) at 410 East 62nd Street, New York, New York, 10021, also offers editions of especially commissioned prints to its membership at prices much less than normal. The Print Club of Philadelphia, 1614 Latimer Street, Philadelphia, Pennsylvania, has been active in the field for many years and publishes small editions of prints, with a preferential price to its members. Many other non-profit societies and groups offer prints to a select group, usually at a distinct price advantage over the normal commercial channels.

Many museums offer prints to the public which are not available through commercial galleries or dealers. The sponsoring institution can not guarantee the immortality of any of its selections but, as the panel which chooses the print to be published is likely to be composed of experts the chances are that their choice will have some validity, at least.

Auctions and special sales are usually publicized in local newspapers. These may contain many worthwhile impressions but the buyer is completely on his own, as items purchased can rarely be returned. A collector may locate other collectors who will either sell or trade prints in order to build a collection in a certain field. Many publishers are releasing portfolios and deluxe volumes of illustrated books which contain fine prints, usually at a reasonable price because of the number of prints involved. The collecting of fine books which contain original prints is an area which combines literature and the visual arts in a particularly satisfying way.

How To Show and Store Prints

Most collectors display only a portion of their treasures on the walls. Like the tip of an iceberg, these may just indicate the bulk of the work stored in cabinets or closets. Color prints, especially, should be displayed only in subdued light, preferably away from reflected sunlight, and should not be left on display for extended periods of time. All colors will eventually change if exposed to bright light. The careful collector will be content to view his most brilliant color pieces at intervals.

Prints should touch only 100% rag mounts and should be hung from the back portion of the mount with non-staining

Prints can be stored vertically or horizontally in Romano-Ross workshop. Shelves are spaced three to six inches apart.

Permanent storage of prints can be obtained by using solander cases, with dust proof lids and spring catches.

hinges. Cardboard mats are not necessary, except for very large prints (over 30″) because they bulk up the collection and take up too much room. Heavy paper will suffice for most prints of small and medium size. These may be stored flat in solander cases, which are dustproof and have positive spring latches to close the lid. Portfolios are good when they have flaps to keep out dust and if they are closed tightly to prevent warping. They are not as good as solander cases for long term storage.

When prints are to be displayed on walls, they should be covered with glass to protect them from dust and dirt. The edges of the glass should be protected by a frame and the back sealed. The surface of the print should not touch the glass because condensation on the inside of the frame might cause water staining. This can be achieved with a suitable mat or strips to separate the print from the glass.

Patented brackets and other devices are good for temporary display of prints and should not be used as permanent fixtures. Dimensional prints need special boxes, often made of plastic, which scratches from the continual cleaning necessary to keep the dust away. Sheet plastic has a curious magnetic quality which attracts dust. Very large prints are difficult to store and need large cabinets or strong crates to keep them. Some may be rolled and kept in cardboard tubes. As a collection grows it may need its own room, which should have a large work table, good general illumination, and a movable small lamp for close examination of prints. A magnifying glass of 8 or 10 power is a help when studying some prints.

THE DEALER AND THE EDITION

As there are many more dealers and distributors who handle prints or purchase individual prints and editions outright than there were 10 years ago, it is much easier now for an artist to find an outlet for selling his work. However, certain pitfalls are worth mentioning. Usually the beginning artist leaves a group of his prints on consignment with the dealer for sale at a specified commission. The percentage that the dealer takes can vary from one third to one half. If the dealer wants your work badly enough, he will sometimes arrange an outright purchase of a number of works at a discounted price. Such a sale can be desirable for the artist in most cases. Distributors of prints will often buy whole editions from an artist at a greatly reduced price, which can vary from 10% or 15% to 30% of the price of the print. The attraction of a large sum of money must be weighed against the time it takes to produce the print.

When an artist leaves work on consignment, he should prepare duplicate sheets with a simply stated agreement specifying amount of commission, his request for monthly payment for work sold, and his request to be able to withdraw his work from the dealer on demand. A listing of prints should then follow, with edition numbers and selling prices. The dealer should be presented with two copies to sign, one for the dealer, one for the artist. Some years ago the Print Council of America, 527 Madison Avenue, New York City, prepared such a form as a guide for artists. It was very useful to us when we began working with numerous dealers.

Investigate all small out-of-town dealers. You can ask for the names of artists handled by the dealer and contact them to inquire about the dealer's working arrangements and general reputation. Remember, it is difficult to retrieve work once it is shipped to distant cities and much easier to do a little investigating before you are involved. Too many artists have suffered badly at the hands of unscrupulous dealers or just from dealers who sold their galleries intact with consignment work to new owners who may or may not be ethical.

RECORD-KEEPING

Unfortunately the very system of edition-making requires some kind of record-keeping. The artist, like the grocery store owner, is dealing with an inventory, and the inventory is his prints. Use the simplest method possible for a very dull job. We generally hate this aspect of printmaking but unfortunately it is necessary. Our system is to keep two large looseleaf notebooks of different colors, one book for noting editions, where sold, where consigned, and the date, and one book to hold agreements and print listings from each gallery, all placed alphabetically (by print titles) in the books. When a print is sold it is checked off in the edition book and in the gallery listing book. This system is fairly accurate. A separate listing of exhibitions where you exhibit each year is also helpful so that a record of the print shown, date and place of show can be made.

SIZE OF EDITION

The handling, signing, numbering, and cataloging of the prints is difficult because the print is produced in a multiple edition. Each print is unique, yet part of a designed quantity of prints called an edition. A similar situation exists in the making of a limited edition of castings by the sculptor; however, such castings are not always numbered.

The printing of the edition itself may be handled in a variety of ways, depending on the probable demand for a print, the ease of printing, and whether the edition is printed by the artist or by a printer for artists. The artist decides on the number to be printed unless a dealer in prints commissions an edition and designates the number for the edition. The usual number for an artist-printed edition used to be 25 or 50. However, so many changes have occurred in the last few years with the appearance of numerous new print galleries and publishers and distributors, coupled with a general increase in demand for prints, that the number of prints in an edition has drastically increased. Editions of 200 to 300 prints are produced quite regularly, and some artists have been known to sign up to 2000 prints, printed by professional artist printers and produced as special editions.

The size of the edition used to be kept small in order to insure the value of each print and hopefully to raise the price of each one as the edition sold out. However, with the wide distribution and demand for the print today it is impossible to speculate on supply and demand in relation to size of edition.

Some artists decide on the size of the edition but do not print the whole number immediately. They may print 10 or 15 to start with, numbering the first group 1 through 15, for an edition of say 50, record the number printed in a book, and then fill out the rest of the edition when they have more printing time or can engage assistants or give out the remainder of the edition to a printer for artists. We often prefer this method for our complicated color collagraphs so that we can be free for new work. A very accurate, detailed printing chart must be kept so that the edition can be filled out exactly as it began. This system has worked very well for us because our diagrams are very good and v*re supplement them with color saved in wax paper packages and recipes for color mixtures. This method is discussed at length in the chapter on the collagraph.

Other artists prefer to print their whole edition immediately to free themselves from reprinting. Time and experience will determine the method best suited to your work. Of course the deferred-printing system cannot work for lithography or for silk screen. For lithography the stones would be difficult to store, and silk-screen printing is a relatively fast printing technique that allows for fairly easy edition work. Interrupted printing applies best to relief and intaglio printing.

A number of artists feel that the limited-edition numbering system protects only the dealer and the collector at the expense of the artist and refuse to use the system. Instead, they sign the prints and mark them as artist's proofs or only sign them.

When an edition is complete, the blocks, plates, screens, stones, or whatever contains the image should be destroyed or defaced. This precaution against further reproduction is usually requested when editions are commissioned. It is done in many cases by scratching, cutting, or drawing a line through the printing surface. However some unscrupulous dealers have attained possession of plates and then proceeded to print them and sell them unsigned and defaced. Many important 19th- and 20th-century French artists' prints may be found along the Quais in Paris or in small dealer's shops in this condition.

Occasionally an artist prints his edition, retains the blocks or plates, and decides at a later time to pull new prints. The artist may alter his color relationships or perhaps even make structural changes. Any editions pulled from altered blocks or plates should be designated as second editions.

NUMBERING, TITLING, AND SIGNING

The numbering, titling, and signing of the edition has traditionally been done with a medium pencil on the bottom of the print. The number of the print and the size of the edition are written on its lower left side with the designation 1/50 for the first print of an edition of fifty, 2/50 for the second, and so on until 50/50 is numbered. The title is usually written in the bottom center and the artist's signature in the lower right. Whether the edition is printed all at once or over a period of time, the prints should be printed as much the same as possible. The numbering then designates the sequence in time and not prime value for low numbers and less value for higher numbers. Probably the question most asked by laymen is whether print number 1 is more valuable than print number 50. Many artists avoid the whole problem by simply writing edition 50 in the lower left corner of each print. However, the traditional method of individual numbering does afford the artist an accurate bookkeeping device if he sends out many prints to exhibitions.

ARTIST'S PROOFS

Traditionally, 10% of an edition should be designated *artist's proofs*. These prints are of the same quality as the numbered edition and are designated as artist's proofs because they are the prints retained by the artist if an entire edition is sold outright or printed and sold one by one. If an edition is sold outright at a discounted price, the artist's proofs will sell at the artist's usual selling price or more, at the discretion of the artist if the edition is sold.

Artist's proofs are also numbered with Roman numerals like I/X and XX/XX or with a system of letters, A, B, C, and so on.

Years ago it was customary for collectors to covet artist's proofs, most often because in the French tradition of print-making the artist worked closely with a printer and inspected the proofs submitted by the printer and marked his choice "bon a tirer" and signed the print as guide for the edition. As these collectors felt this print was the first to meet the artist's approval, it was therefore more desirable. Because artists now print editions themselves and give equal care to the first and the last prints in an edition, this fixation on the artist's proof as the most accurate state has diminished.

WORKING PROOFS

During the early stages of the development of the print the artist may experiment with a number of color combinations, different wipings, or rolling, and the like. Though these prints may not be the final choice for the edition, they often contain many interesting variations and should be marked working proofs and numbered in the sequence pulled. These prints will no doubt have value as an edition is depleted and, more importantly, are of considerable value in studying the development of a print. If you have ever had the opportunity to see the numerous stages of many of Rembrandt's etchings that can be studied, you will understand how interesting the working proofs of an artist can be for the total comprehension of a work of art.

THE RESTRIKE

A restrike is a print that has been pulled from a block or plate at a much later date than the original printing. Many restrikes exist of Rembrandt etchings, pulled in the 18th and 19th centuries. Numerous restrike prints exist of work by Goya and Kollwitz. Such impressions may be inferior to the prints printed in the artist's lifetime. Sometimes the plates are reworked, usually being steel-faced in order to obtain long runs. When the prints are sold as restrikes at modest prices they are often interesting to study and to own. When the restrikes are sold as artist-pulled proofs for large sums, it is most unfortunate for the unsuspecting buyer. The best advice in this area would be to always buy from a reputable dealer and be wary of "fantastic" buys in master prints. Finding such a buy is highly unlikely.

RAPHAEL · VRBINAS ·

Ugo Da Carpi
"The Descent from the Cross," after Raphael
Chiaroscuro Woodcut
The Metropolitan Museum of Art
Rogers Fund, 1922

Seong Moy
"View from the Window, Yellow Sun"
Relief print 24½" x 20"
Courtesy of the artist

SOURCES AND CHARTS

SOURCES OF SUPPLIES FOR PRINTMAKING

General Supplies (tools, paper, ink, and so on)

Craftool Company
1 Industrial Road
Woodridge, New Jersey 07075

Sam Flax
25 East 28 Street
New York, New York 10016
(Also in Chicago, Los Angeles, San Francisco, and Sacramento)

Arthur Brown
2 West 46 Street
New York, New York

Fine Arts Materials Co.
531 LaGuardia Place
New York, New York

Rembrandt Graphic Arts Co.
Stockton, New Jersey 08559

F. Weber Co. (order from local dealers)
Wayne and Windrim Avenue
Philadelphia, Pennsylvania 19144

Graphic Chemical & Ink Co.
P. O. Box 27
728 North Yale Avenue
Villa Park, Illinois 60181

Cherry or Poplar Type-High Blocks:

Reliance Blocking
9419 Railroad Avenue
North Bergen, New Jersey

American Wood Type Co.
42–25 9th Street
Long Island City, New York

Birch Plywood from Finland:

Stewart Industries
6520 North Hoyne Avenue
Chicago, Illinois 60645

End-Grain Maple or Boxwood Blocks:

J. Johnson & Co.
33 Matincock Ave.
Port Washington
New York, 11050

Tools (gouges, knives, chisels, stones, and so on)

E. C. Lyons
16 West 22 Street
New York, New York 10011

E. C. Mueller
3646 White Plains Road
Bronx, New York 10467

Frank Mittermeier, Inc.
3577 E. Tremont Avenue
Bronx, New York 10465

Sculpture Associates
114 East 25th St.
New York, New York

Wilfred C. Kimber, Ltd.
24 King's Bench Street
Blackfriars
London, S.E.1, England
(also Hunter, Penrose, Littlejohn Ltd.)

Felt Blankets

Continental Felt Co.
22 West 15th Street
New York, New York

Pacific States Felt & Mfg. Co.
843 Howard Street
San Francisco, California 94103

Pigments (for ink and paint):

Fezandie & Sperrle Inc.
103 Lafayette Street
New York, New York 10013

Interchemical Printing Corp.
16th and Willow
Oakland, California

E. I. DuPont De Nemours Co.
Pigments Department
Wilmington, Delaware

Acids and Chemicals:

Amend Drug and Chemical Co.
83 Cordier Street
Irvington, New Jersey

City Chemical Co.
132 West 22 St.
New York, New York

Philip Hunt Co.
707 Army Street
San Francisco, California 94124

for Gentry Clove Oil:
Beacon Chemical Co.
244 Lafayette Street
New York, N. Y. 10012

Photoengraving Supplies, Including Copper Brass, and Zinc Plates:

Harold Pitman Co.
515 Secaucus Road
Secaucus, New Jersey 07094

Bond Metal Supply Co.
321 Canal St.
New York, N. Y.

For small quantities:
National Steel & Copper Plate Co.
653 10th Avenue
New York, N. Y.

Rollers and Brayers:

Apex Roller Co.
1541 No. 16 Street
St. Louis, Missouri

Ideal Roller Co.
21 39th Avenue
Long Island City, New York

Jomac, Inc.
181 Broad Street
Carlstadt, New Jersey

Speedball Soft Rubber Brayers
Hunt Manufacturing Co.
Statesville, North Carolina
(Many local dealers)

Cylinder Rubber (for rollers)

Miller Products Co.
29 Warren Street
New York, New York

Printing Ink (letterpress):

IPI (Interchem Corp.) (Everyday Ink)
636 11 Avenue
New York, New York

Siebold Ink Co.
150 Varick Street
New York City, New York

Sun Chemical Corp.
General Printing Ink
750 3rd Avenue
New York, New York 10017

Paper:

large stock of imported and domestic papers:
Andrews/Nelson/Whitehead
7 Laight Street (on Canal St.)
New York, New York 10013

for white index and cover stock:
Crestwood Paper Corp.
263 9th Avenue
New York, New York

tableau paper in sheets and rolls:
Technical Paper Corp.
729 Boylston Street
Boston, Massachusetts 02116

cover stock, blotters
Saxon Paper Co.
240 West 18th Street
New York, New York

Corrugated board in quantity:
Standard Corrugated & Case Corp.
686 Grand Avenue
Ridgefield, N. J. 07657

West coast dealer for A/N/W
Zellerbach Paper Co.
234 South Spruce Street
South San Francisco, California 94118

Mat, chipboard in quantity:
Miller Cardboard Co.
80–82 Wooster Street
New York, New York

Fine Arts Material Co.

Handmade Japanese papers:
Yasutomo & Co.
Dept. AA-4 24 California Street
San Francisco, California 94111

Japanese papers and tools:
Aiko
714 North Wabash
Chicago, Illinois

for blotters, commercial cover stock:
Lindenmeyer, Schlosser Corp.
5301 11th Street
New York, New York

for Kizuki-bosho paper, used by Uchimai
Shimizu-Seirindo
8–1, Honmachi Nihonbashi,
Chuo-ku, Tokyo, Japan

Photographic Techniques

For Kodak KPR Chemicals & Ortho Film:
Treck Photographic Inc.
1 West 39th Street
New York, New York 10018

For Print-E-Mulsion & SC 12 Superfast:
Rockland Colloid Corp.
599 River Road
Piermont, New York 10968

Plastic Sheets

Commercial Plastic & Supply Corp.
630 Broadway
New York, New York
or local supplier

Benelux Press Beds

Laminated Sheet Products
Industrial Park Corporation
Norwood, Massachussetts

Asbestos Machine Corp.
23–24 McDonald Ave.
Brooklyn, New York

Hard Ground (mixed with lacquer thinner)

Heims Etching Ground
John L. Heim
1205 Virginia Avenue
Glendale 2, Calif.
(Available from Cronite Co.)

Steel Facing of Copper Plates

Anderson & Lamb
Fulton Street
Brooklyn, New York

CANADIAN SUPPLIERS

Artist's Supplies, Papers, Inks

Heinz Jordan & Co., Ltd.
42 Gladstone Ave.
Toronto 3, Ontario, Canada

Inks

E. Harris Co., Ltd.
1397 Odlum Drive
Vancouver, British Columbia

Chemicals

Christie Chemical Co.
7995 14th Avenue, St. Michel
Montreal 455, Quebec, Canada

Fine Papers

Coast Paper
798 Beatty Street
Vancouver, British Columbia

Etching Press

Zimmcor Artmetwork, Inc.
6120 Metropolitan East
Montreal 451, Quebec, Canada

PAPERS FOR PRINTMAKING

Name	Size (in.)	Composition	Intaglio	Litho	Relief	Silk Screen	Notes
American Etching	38 x 50	100% rag, machine-made.	x	x		x	Large size for intaglio plates. White, soft finish, prints well.
Arches Cover	22 x 30 29 x 41	90% rag, mould-made.	x	x	x	x	Available in white and buff; smooth, even, beautiful texture. Handsome finish.
Arches Text	25 x 40	90% rag, mould-made.	x	x	x	x	Light, even, white, laid and wove finish.
Basingwerk Heavy	26 x 40	45% Esparto pulp, machine-made.	x	x	x	x	Very smooth, even surface. Good for proofs. Inexpensive, useful paper.
Beckett Cover	26 x 40	25% rag, machine-made.	x	x	x	x	Inexpensive, smooth, brilliant white permanent paper, very useful.
Classico Watercolor	22 x 30	100% rag, mould-made.	x				Beautiful, heavy, handsome, white, textured, expensive, for intaglio prints.
Copperplate	22 x 30 30 x 42	33% rag, mould-made.	x	x	x	x	Soft, white. Fragile when damp and should be handled with care. Prints well.
Copperplate Deluxe	22 x 30 30 x 42	75% rag, mould-made.	x	x	x	x	Permanent, white, soft, needs little dampening to soften fibres, expensive.
Crisbrook Etching	22 x 31	100% rag, handmade.	x	x	x	x	Soft, white, unsized. Prints well. Fairly expensive.
Domestic Etching	26 x 40	50% rag, machine-made.	x	x	x	x	Cheap, white, useful paper.
English Etching	22 x 31	100% rag, mould-made.	x	x	x	x	White, nice texture, moderately priced, handsome sheet.
German Etching	22 x 30 30 x 42	75% rag, mould-made.	x	x	x	x	Beautiful finish, soft, white, even, moderately expensive.
Goyu	21 x 29	Part Kozo, handmade.	x	x		x	Thin, off-white, even texture. Prints delicate detail well.
Hosho	19 x 24	Part Kozo, handmade.	x	x	x	x	White, soft, small sheet, good for color woodcuts. Picks up fluff on press.
Hosho (student)	16 x 22	Part Kozo, handmade.		x	x	x	Cheap, uneven, small, good for student proofs.
Hosho Pure	—	Part Kozo, handmade.	x	x	x	x	Expensive, beautiful, strong off-white handsome sheet. Available only from Japan.
Index	26 x 40	100% sulphite pulp, machine-made.	x	x	x	x	Cheap proof paper. Strong, white, turns brittle with age.
Inomachi (Nacre)	20 x 26	100% Kozo, handmade.	x	x	x	x	Elegant threaded texture. Prints etchings well but must be carefully dampened. Expensive.
Italia	20 x 28 28 x 40	67% rag, mould-made.	x	x	x	x	White, soft, handsome finish. Moderately priced. Does not erase well.
Iyo Glazed	17 x 22	Part Kozo, handmade.		x	x	x	Uneven texture, white, small sheet, inexpensive.
J. Green Watercolor	27 x 40	100% rag, mould-made.	x	x	x	x	Nice texture, warm white, prints well, handsome sheet.
Kizuki-bosho	17 x 24 25 x 35	100% Kozo, handmade.	x	x	x	x	Sized on both sides, for Japanese method with water-based inks. Made by same family for seven generations.

Paper	Size	Composition						Description
Kochi	20 x 26	Part Kozo, handmade.				x	x	Warm off-white, handsome finish, elegant look, moderately priced, uneven thickness.
Masa 225	21 x 31	Manila and sulphite, machine-made.			x	x	x	Cheap, flecked, natural color, good for black-and-white proofs. Not permanent.
Millbourn 140 lb.	22 x 30	100% rag, handmade.	x			x	x	Expensive, beautiful, lovely texture. Strong white. A handsome sheet.
Mohawk Text	26 x 40	100% sulphite, machine-made.	x	x		x	x	Cheap, proving paper only.
Moriki 1009	25 x 36	Kozo, handmade				x	x	White, soft, unsized, useful paper.
Moriki (colors)	25 x 36	Kozo, handmade				x	x	Many beautiful colors. Soft, unsized, moderately priced.
Mulberry	24 x 33	Part Kozo, handmade.	x			x	x	Thin, off-white, tears easily. Not expensive. Good for general woodcut printing.
Mulberry Student	24 x 33	Sulphite, handmade.				x	x	Cheap paper for proofs and student work.
Murillo	27 x 39	33% rag, mould-made.	x				x	Very heavy, strong, buff color, even texture, good for deep intaglio and very sensitive.
Okawara	36 x 72	Kozo, handmade.				x	x	Very large, natural tan color, fairly opaque, even texture, handsome finish.
Opaline Parchment	22 x 28	100% sulphite, machine-made.				x	x	Smooth, even finish. Good for wood engravings and delicate relief prints. Discolors.
Pericles Cover	26 x 40	Rag and sulphite, machine-made.	x	x		x	x	Fairly permanent, white, smooth, even, good for silk-screen editions.
Rives Heavy	19 x 26 26 x 40	100% rag, mould-made.	x	x		x	x	White, slight texture, not heavy enough for deep embossing, but very useful.
Rives BFK	22 x 30 29 x 41	100% rag, mould-made.	x	x		x	x	A standard paper with many uses. White, even smooth texture, almost opaque. A classic paper.
Sekishu	24 x 39	Kozo, handmade.				x	x	Two colors available, white and natural, thin, soft, inexpensive, tears easily.
Strathmore Artists	—	100% rag, machine-made.	x	x			x	Strong, white sheet with monotonous texture.
Suzuki	36 x 72	Part Kozo, handmade.				x	x	Very large, white, slight texture. Good for large woodcuts, medium weight.
Tableau	40″ rolls	Machine-made.		x		x	x	Unlimited length, very tough, will not discolor, used as a filter paper. Available in cut sheets.
Torinoko	21 x 31	Part manila hemp.				x	x	Strong, white, opaque, expensive, nice texture.
Troya #40	24 x 36	Hemp, machine-made.				x	x	Cheap, smooth, even paper, good for proofs. Will discolor to pale brown, turns brittle with age.
Tuscan Cover	26 x 40	100% sulphite, machine-made.	x	x		x	x	Good for etching proofs, is cheap, smooth, turns brittle with age.

Note: Esparto is a grass fiber. Kozo is a plant fiber.

Only the books and articles that might be useful to a working artist-printmaker are included. The literature on prints and printmaking is vast, and works that are essentially scholarly in nature are listed separately. The tabulation of monographs on individual artists is listed alphabetically by artist and is intended as source material to reveal what some of the most inspired artists throughout the centuries have done with the creative print. In general, emphasis is placed on works that are currently available as reprints.

General

Eichenberg, Fritz (editor), *Artists Proof* (Magazine and Annuals), All issues, Pratt Graphic Art Center, New York. The most complete and best-produced survey of contemporary printmaking.

Getlein, Frank and Dorothy, *The Bite of the Print*, Clarkson N. Potter, Inc., New York 1963. A sympathetic and enthusiastic outline of satire and irony in prints.

Gilmour, Pat, *Modern Prints*, Studio Vista|Dutton Pictureback, London, 1970. A small format survey of contemporary prints.

Hayter, Stanley William, *About Prints*, Oxford University Press, London 1962. A innovator in contemporary printmaking discusses some aspects of the field.

Ivins, William, *How Prints Look*, Beacon Hill, paperback 1943. Analysis and enlargements of techniques by an expert.

Ivins, William, *Prints and Visual Communication*, DaCapo reprint, New York 1969. Some fascinating insights into prints as information bearers.

Karshan, Donald, *American Printmaking*, Smithsonian Institution Press 1969. A readable, historical survey.

Karshan, Donald, *Language of the Print*, Chanticleer Press, New York, Random House, 1968. Selections from a remarkable, recently acquired collection of master prints.

Mayor, A. Hyatt, *Prints and People*, Metropolitan Museum of Art, New York 1971. A brilliant and witty survey of prints, written with great style by the Curator Emeritus of the Metropolitan.

Roger-Marx, Claude, *Graphic Art of the Nineteenth Century*, McGraw-Hill, New York 1962. Informative, brilliant discussion of an intensely interesting period in printmaking. Small format.

Sachs, Paul J., *Modern Prints and Drawings*, Knopf, New York 1954. Small format, readable, well-chosen illustrations.

Sotriffer, Kristan, *Printmaking, History and Technique*, McGraw-Hill, New York 1968. A good, general introduction to the history of printmaking. Some worthwhile illustrations.

Zigrosser, Carl, *The Book of Fine Prints*, Crown Publishers, New York 1956. A classic short history of printmaking. Clear, readable text, small reproductions.

Zigrosser, Carl, *Multum in Parvo*, G. Braziller, New York 1965. An appreciation of miniature prints.

General Techniques

Brunner, Felix, *A Handbook of Graphic Reproduction Processes*, Visual Communication Books, Hastings House, New York. Highly useful. Good layout and design.

Heller, Jules, *Printmaking Today*, University of Southern California 1965, Revised 1971. Elementary survey of print techniques.

Peterdi, Gabor, *Printmaking*, Macmillan 1971. Recently updated, this is one of the most useful books on the intaglio processes by a creative and innovative artist.

Relief Print Techniques

Green, Peter, *Introducing Surface Printing*, Watson-Guptill, New York 1967. Lots of pictorial material and good ideas about the relief print.

Green, Peter, *New Creative Printmaking*, Watson-Guptill, New York 1964. Excellent for its uninhibited approach to new forms in printmaking.

Karshan, Donald, *Picasso Linocuts 1958–1963*, Tudor, New York. A lucid explanation of a remarkable new approach to the color linocut.

Kent, Cyril and Cooper, Mary, *Simple Printmaking*, Watson-Guptill, New York, 1966. Intended for children but is useful for all beginning students.

Mueller, Hans A., *Woodcuts and Wood-engravings and How I Make Them*, Pynson Printers, New York 1939. A popular illustrator of the 30's and a fine craftsman talks about his approach.

Rothenstein, Michael, *Frontiers of Printmaking*, Reinhold, New York 1966. Introduction to some contemporary solutions to print problems.

Rothenstein, Michael, *Linocuts and Woodcuts*, Watson-Guptill, New York 1963. A highly respected teacher presents some new approaches.

Rothenstein, Michael, *Relief Printing*, Watson-Guptill, New York 1970. A really fresh and creative view of relief printmaking.

Japanese Woodcuts

Binyon and Sexton, *Japanese Colour Prints*, Frederick Publications 1954. Much information in a tiny format, including publisher seals.

Gentoles, Margaret, *Masters of the Japanese Print*, Asia Society, Harry Abrams, New York 1964. Paperback catalog of a distinguished exhibition at Asia House, New York.

Hillier, J., *Utamaro*, Phaidon, London 1961. A giant of Japanese prints.

Michener, James, *The Floating World*, Random House, New York 1954. A popularized but worthwhile account of the Japanese print. Poor reproductions.

Robertson, Ronald, *Contemporary Printmaking in Japan*, Crown Publishers, New York 1965. An analysis of how the new wave of Japanese printmakers has expanded the traditional procedures.

Yoshida, Toshi and Rei Yuki, *Japanese Printmaking, a handbook of traditional and modern techniques*, Charles E. Tuttle Co., Rutland, Vermont, and Tokyo. A thorough and definitive study of Japanese water-based techniques.

Monographs on Artists
(Listed alphabetically by artist)

Leonard Baskin, The Graphic Work 1950–60, FAR Gallery, New York 1970.

Bonnard Lithographe, by Claude Roger-Marx, Andre Sauret, Monte Carlo 1952.

Georges Braque; His Graphic Work, by W. Hofmann, Harry Abrams, New York.

Bresdin, Rodolphe, by K. G. Boon, Amsterdam 1955. A fantacist of the highest rank whose lithographs are well worth study.

Graphic Works of Peter Brueghel the Elder, by A. Klein, Paperback Dover 1963.

Jacques Callot, by Edwin De. T. Bechtel, Braziller, New York 1955.

The Graphic Art of Mary Cassat, by Donald Karshan, Smithsonian Institution 1967.

Marc Chagall, His Graphic Work, by Franz Meyer, Harry Abrams, New York.

The Fantastic Engravings of Wendel Dietterlin, Dover reprint, paperback. Inventive, baroque architectural studies.

Durer, Complete Engravings, Etchings, and Woodcuts, by Karl-Adolf Knappe, Harry Abrams, New York.

The Graphic Art of M. C. Escher, Meredith Press 1961. A craftsman of the first rank creates some ingenious illusions with incredible precision.

Der Liebesspiegel (Gavarni), by E. Wieser, Aehren Verlag Affaltern 1953.

Goya Caprichos, by M. Micko, Spring Books, London.

Complete Etchings of Goya, Crown, New York 1943.

Wood Engravings of Winslow Homer, by B. Gelman, Crown, New York 1969.

Kirchner, His Graphic Art, by Annemarie Dube-Heynig, New York Graphic Society 1961. Many well-printed, large color plates.

Prints and Drawings of Kathe Kollwitz, by Carl Zigrosser, Dover, paperback, 1969.

Marino Marini, Graphic Work and Paintings, Harry Abrams, New York.

Joan Miro, His Graphic Work, by Sam Hunter, Harry Abrams, New York.

Rolf Nesch, Universe Books, New York 1969. A presentation of the work of a fresh creative spirit.

The Graphic Art of Rolf Nesch, Detroit Institute Arts 1969 paperback. Excellent catalog covers a retrospective of the innovator of collage prints.

Pablo Picasso: Fifty-five years of his graphic work, Harry Abrams, New York 1965.

Picasso: Sixty Years of Graphic Works, Introductions by D-H Kahnweiler and B. Geiser, Los Angeles County Mus. of Art paper. Catalog of a large exhibition, well illustrated.

Jose Guadalupe Posada, Hans Secker, Verlag der Kunst Dresden 1961.

Odilon Redon, by Andre Mellerio, Da Capo Press New York 1968. Reprint of a standard work.

The Graphic Works of Odilon Redon, Dover, paperback New York 1969.

Rembrandt, by K. G. Boon, Harry Abrams. Good reproductions.

The Complete Engravings of Martin Schongauer, by Alan Shestack, Dover paperback 1969.

E. Vuillard, L'Oeuvre Gravé, by Claude Roger Marx, Andre Sauret, Monte Carlo 1952.

Ward, Lynd, God's Man, A Novel in Woodcuts, Johnathan Cape and Harrison Smith, New York 1929.

Scholarly Treatises

Delteil, Loys, *Le Peintre-Graveur Illustre'*, Collector's Editions, New York Reprint of 32 columes, Major work of 19th-century and early 20th-century French artists.

Dortu, M. G., *Toulouse-Lautrec et son oeuvre*, Collector's Editions, New York 1970 6 volume reprint.

Harris, Jean, *Edouard Manet, Graphic Works: A Definite Catalogue Raisonne*, Collector's Editions, New York 1970 reprint.

Hind, Arthur M., *A Catalog of Rembrandt's Etchings*, Da Capo reprint in two volumes. 1967.

Hind, Arthur M., *A History of Engraving and Etching from the 15th century* to 1914, Dover reprint, paperback. Many astute observations and evaluations.

Hind, Arthur M., *An Introduction to the History of Woodcut*, Dover reprint, in two volumes, paperback.

Hollstein, F. W. H., *Dutch & Flemish Etchings, Engravings & Woodcuts, 1450–1700*, Menno Hertzberger, Amsterdam, various dates in 19 volumes. A detailed survey of an enormous body of work.

Hallstein, F. W. H., *German Engravings, Etchings &*

Woodcuts 1400–1700, Menno Hertzberger, Amsterdam, various dates in 7 volumes. A thorough and effective study of the scene. A monumental work.

Laran, *Jean, L'Estampe*, Presses Universitaires de France, 1959 in 2 volumes. Beautifully printed, with large heliogravure and color reproductions.

Lehrs, Max, *History and Critical Catalog of German, Netherlandish and French Copper Engravings in the 15th Century*, Collector's Edition, New York 1970. Reprint of 9 volumes.

Lehrs, Max, *Late Gothic Engravings of Germany and the Netherlands*, Dover paperback 1969. Marvelous source material for this era.

Lieure, Jules, *Jacques Callot: La Vie Artisique et Catalogue Raissone*, Collectors Editions, New York 1970. Reprint of 9 volumes.

Massar, Phyllis Dearborn, *Stefano della Bella: Catalogue Raisonne*, Collectors Edition reprint, New York 1970—two volumes.

Minott, Charles I., *The Engravings of Martin Schongauer: Studies and Illustrated Catalogue*, Collectors Edition Reprint, New York 1970.

Mourlot, Fernand, *Picasso Lithographe 1919–1956*, Monte Carlo: Andre Sauret 1949–1964 4 vols. Beautifully printed but rare and expensive because original lithos are included.

Panofsky, Erwin, *Albecht Durer*, Princeton, 1943 2 vols. The definitive study of Durer and his work.

INDEX

D

WELLS BINDERY, INC.

OCT   1978

WALTHAM, MASS. 02154